Adopting In Russia:

Your Rights and the Law

Adopting In Russia:

Your Rights and the Law

Irina Mikhailovna O'Rear
Russian Attorney

Copyright 2002
All Rights Reserved

Published by:
RUSSIA LEGAL PRESS

Adopting In Russia:

Your Rights and the Law

ISBN: 0-9722376-0-7

Printed in the United States of America

First Edition – August 2002

INTRODUCTION

This book has been written in order to provide the reader with basic and helpful information pertaining to Russian Adoptions and Russian Adoption Law. Although the laws are translated from Russian into English, this translated version provides you with a comprehensive view of these laws and your rights surrounding Foreign Adoption.

Because of the complexity of issues that surround each and every Russian Adoption, and because Russian Laws are quite specific as they apply to the adoption process, these laws should be understood as the basis or foundation of the decision process. These laws are the starting point. Of course, as with any court of law, it is the Judge's responsibility to apply the law to each case and to act in the best interest of the child. If the Court determines that for any reason the adoption is not in the best interest of a child, the Judge can and will rule accordingly. However, it is always the right of the adoptive parent or parents to appeal any Court decision should an adoption not be granted.

This book is intended to serve as a resource and reference guide for those pursuing an adoption through Russia. This book will be helpful to those families adopting with the assistance of an agency, as well as to those adopting independently. It will answer many of the common questions as well as provide the reader with reliable information on the adoption processes, including the portions of the actual translated (Russian to English) Russian Law surrounding foreign adoption. The accuracy of information provided in this book is intended to be current as of the date of publication. Any opinions given in this book are strictly those of the author.

FORWARD AND DEDICATION

I am a licensed Russian Attorney and former Russian Judge. Since leaving Russia I have devoted my professional life to helping individuals and families from around the world fulfill their dreams of adding a child or children to their loving family.

I am motivated by the many thousands of beautiful, deserving and innocent orphan children who are in desperate need of a loving family. I have had the pleasure of working with many wonderful people seeking to adopt from Russia. There have been families with no children who are unable to conceive biologically and single parent-hopefuls as well as those who already have a large family but see the need and have the desire to extend their family to bring a needy child into their loving home. In each case I have found people with their own personal reasons for wanting to adopt, but there is also in each some commonalities: the love of children, the desire to "save" a child from life's harsh uncertainties, the need to provide a safe and nurturing environment for children and the personal courage to step forward responsibly.

It is to these loving, dedicated families and individuals and the precious, needy children of Russia that I dedicate this book.

TABLE OF CONTENTS

<u>Chapter</u>   **<u>Page</u>**

TABLE OF CONTENTS

TABLE OF CONTENTS

TABLE OF CONTENTS

"...the child, for the full and harmonious development of his or her personality, should grow up in a family environment, in an atmosphere of happiness, love and understanding..."

The Convention of the Rights of the Children

Chapter One

Making Your Decision

This book begins with what I believe to be the most important chapter. The decision to adopt can be daunting, and the decision to adopt from a country you probably know very little about may well be frightening. No one should make this kind of decision without a great deal of thought and research. You may wish to begin your decision process with the basic question of why adopt, then move on to the more interesting questions of why from Russia. So then,

Why Adopt?

Coming to the decision to adopt is an intensely personal process. I have heard everything from "We are unable to have children ourselves" to "This is what God wants us to do." Whatever the reasons, I believe that most people are well intentioned and genuine in their motivations to add that special child or children to their loving family. While I cannot answer this all-important question specifically for anyone, I would like to provide some "food for thought" for those exploring this wonderful alternative to expand their families. I encourage you to continue to explore your own reasons and motivations as you go through the process. The insights you gain from your personal reflections will serve you well and may even give you strength as you travel down the often confusing, difficult and sometimes frustrating international adoption road.

Cultural Views of Adoption

Each culture varies widely on its opinions of adoption. Some cultures consider adoption a wonderful, loving thing to do, a very noble, unselfish gesture of humanity. Other cultures consider this a "dark side" of their society, doing everything possible to hide it and keep it a secret from outsiders. Exploring these varied cultural attitudes may lead us to some understanding of the motivations and the views of others and may offer some insight into this subject for oneself.

Russian Views on Adoption

Russian culture is sort of in the middle on this topic. Russian people can and do pursue adoptions in Russia, usually due to their own inability to have biological children, but Russian adoptive parents are often secretive about their adoptions and tend to keep the facts hidden from society.

More often than not, orphans adopted by Russian families are infants. This way, the family fills a void in their life while maintaining the ability to publicly appear more naturally as biological parents. Some Russian women even go so far as to imitate a pregnancy in order to make this more believable.

Of course, there are other reasons Russian citizens adopt. But the fact is that there is a great difference in the number of children (from infants to children 16 years of age) available for adoption and the number of Russian families adopting. The primary reason there are so many orphaned Russian children is the biological family's financial inability to provide even the minimal care for a child. Most families cannot afford another mouth to feed. As difficult as it is for those of us living in relative affluence to understand, the decision to place a child in the Russian state orphanage system is most often purely an economic decision. The collapse of the former USSR and the multitude of social and economic problems left in its wake has resulted in a vast number of children in orphanages in desperate need of a family.

Loving Parents Needed

Families and individuals who have thoughtfully and carefully made the decision to adopt are much needed in Russia. For those researching adoption for the first time, the most basic question has always been "why do I/we want to adopt?" Once you have soul searched, researched and pondered every aspect of adoption and your final conclusion is that you have sound and valid reasons and desires to adopt, then you have to decide where you want to adopt from.

Why Adopt in Russia?

Russia has been a very popular destination for many families pursuing international adoptions. The number of Americans adopting from Russia has remained fairly constant over the last several years.

*The following information indicates the number of visas issued for orphans adopted from Russia and some former Republics of the USSR (Kazakhstan, Armenia, Azerbaijan, Georgia):

Year	# IR3 Visas	#IR4 Visas	Total Number Visas
1998	4339	172	4511
1999	4442	28	4470
2000	4655	22	4677
2001	4956	58	5014

* Statistics provided by the US Embassy, Moscow. This information only reflects the number of US adoptions from Russia (and former Soviet select countries), statistics for total number of foreign adoptions were not available in its entirety.

*Year by year the total number of children placed for adoption in Russia has decreased. For example, in 1996 the number of adopted children was 30,635, in 1998 it was 25,461, and in 2000 it was 13,700. Among them, Russian citizens adopted 7,400 children and foreign citizens adopted 6,300 children.

* The official statistics from the State report. "About the position of children in the Russian Federation"

Most prospective adoptive families point to certain factors that make Russia more attractive to them than other areas of the world for adoption. Some of these factors include: availability of "desired" children, the relative cost, a perceived faster adoption process, and laws that protect the family.

Once a child has been legally placed in a family, no one can come and take that child away (unless of course there are legal reasons, such as abuse). Parents of children in Russia who give up their parental rights or have their parental rights removed will not be able to interrupt the family at a future date to "claim" their children. You may have heard the horror stories of families in the United States who adopt a child only to have the biological parent to step in and legally "demand" that the child be returned to their custody. This is not only a devastating blow to the adoptive family, but to the child as well. Russian law protects the adoptive family in such cases.

Other Considerations

Before you decide to adopt from Russia, you should take into account many things such as language, culture, distance, costs, representation and other important aspects of the process. These are pretty broad topics and it is worthwhile to have an overview of facts as you proceed with your decision making process.

Language

Language is usually a limited concern for adoptive parents. Infants and very young children have little or no difficulty adapting to English. It can be an initial concern with older children, but usually even older adopted Russian children acquire their new language in time. All children eventually adapt, but one must understand that there will be frustrations that can test a family.

Keep in mind that school-aged children of Russia (even in the poorer regions of the country) are usually as educated, or often times, more educated than many American children of the same age. This is due primarily to the intensity and quality of the Russian educational system in pre-college schooling. The language problem can certainly present some frustration for the child, and even affect their ability to keep up in their new class setting. Unfortunately, there are American teachers who have sometimes labeled foreign speaking children as "slow learners" without basis. Advanced preparation with the child's school and teachers should thwart any misunderstandings. Electronic translators or Russian - English dictionaries can help children, parents and teachers alike (in addition to a lot of patience and encouragement).

Culture and Heritage

Most adoptive parents start out with the intention of maintaining their child's Russian culture and heritage, but then find this intent diminishing with time.

Most adopted children under thirteen years of age eventually lose not only the majority of their memory of Russia and its culture, but also quickly embrace the new culture of the country where they newly reside. It is always up to the adoptive parent how much of the Russian culture they wish to preserve for each child. This should not be a major concern for those that are not sure. Just do what you are comfortable with.

Parents who are considering a Russian adoption should really not concern themselves too much with this aspect. Of course, if you adopt from Russia, it is a good idea to read up on the history and culture as well as learn some basic words and phrases. This will come in handy more than you might imagine. As you learn more of the Russian culture, it is possible that you may uncover hidden desires to work with preserving some of your child's heritage.

Travel

Traveling to Russia can be quite daunting, especially when you consider the reputation that this country had not long ago when it was perceived to be the "enemy" of many nations. While Russia is no longer an enemy, there remain many unknowns for the person that has not been exposed to this vast and distant country. You should take the time to educate yourself about Russia and its culture. Like in anything else in life, the more you learn and become informed, the higher your comfort level will be.

Traveling can also be disruptive to your existing family since in most cases it will take at least two trips to Russia to complete an adoption. If you have children at home, you will need to consider necessary arrangements for their care. Since Russia is so unpredictable, it is a good idea to allow for extra travel time.

Costs

Most people are shocked to learn that adoption in Russia is <u>FREE</u>! The Russian government does not charge any money to Russian citizens or foreigner*s* who wish to adopt a Russian orphan. There are no legal terms in Russia such as "international fees," "overseas fees," "foreign fees," "referral fees," "Court fees," "in-country fees," etc., since legally, these fees do not exist.

The actual costs of adoption can vary widely. The most experienced and savvy adopting families can complete the process for less than $10,000. Others pay upwards of $40,000. The actual cost of your adoption will depend on several factors, including your choice of representation (independent or agency), your dates of travel, luxuries and conveniences you desire during travel, number of people traveling, number of children being adopted, gifts to orphanage personnel and others involved in the process, donations to orphanages (if desired), etc. With a little common sense and intuition, you can minimize your outlay of cash.

One important item to note here: the price you pay does not necessarily have anything to do with the length of the adoption process or the quality of representation. This is governed by other factors that will be discussed later.

Representation

Adopting internationally is a complicated affair. The constantly changing and ever-increasing number of laws and procedures that characterizes the process can be very frustrating and difficult to negotiate. Unless you are very knowledgeable about Russian adoption laws and procedures, you are well advised to hire international adoption professionals to guide you through the process. Two avenues are available to you: using an adoption agency, or pursuing an independent adoption.

Adoption Agencies

Adoption agencies help facilitate the complicated processes for those that are not well versed in the requirements for Russian adoption. They provide the expertise families need to complete their adoptions.

I must emphasize the importance of selecting high quality representation to complete your adoption. While most adoptions are done through adoption agencies, one must be cautious. On March 28, 2000, Russia implemented a requirement that all adoption agencies be "accredited" in order to legally operate in Russia (Regulation of the Government of the Russian Federation # 268). This means that agencies have met the required criteria, by official regulations, to become accredited or "legally sanctioned" by the Russian government to facilitate foreign adoptions in Russia. According to Article 14 of this Regulation, Accredited Adoption Agencies are authorized to provide the following service:

Agencies of foreign organizations: under the established procedure, submit to the appropriate executive body of the subject of the Russian Federation or to the Federal Operator of Databank of Children of the Russian Federation the documents of prospective adoptive parents residing within the territory of the state where the foreign organization is located for selecting the child for adoption, and also to the Court for establishing the adoption decree; get the invitation for prospective adoptive parents to travel to select the child under the established procedure; organize the reception and placement of prospective adoptive parents, render the needed assistance in the execution of adoption, and realize other activities representing the interests of prospective adoptive parents within the Russian Federation authorized by the legislation of the Russian Federation.

Russian Regulations have also been written so that each accredited agency must go through re-accreditation every year.

According to the Ministry of Education of the Russian Federation, there are reports of a few non-accredited adoption agencies attempting to circumvent this accreditation process by operating illegally or under the "umbrella" of an accredited agency. This creates risk and endangers the adoption for those who choose this route. Should problems emerge during the adoption process, it has been quoted by the Ministry of Education of the Russian Federation that the Russian government will not protect the family since it is participating in an illegal act. If you choose to complete your adoption through an agency, demand to see proof that the agency is accredited to operate in the Russian Federation. Any legitimate adoption agency won't hesitate to provide you with this information.

Accredited agencies typically operate in a specific region or in a few specific regions in Russia. If there is a particular region of Russia you desire, it may be best to research the agencies that are operating successfully and legally within that region. An internet search of adoption agencies may be the most efficient way to accomplish this.

Often, families learn about adoption agencies by word of mouth of satisfied clients. While it is always a comfort to hear good things about an agency that you might want to use, it is imperative that you research the agency even further. Ask for references from the agency. Be sure to call each reference and ask about their experience, good and bad. It may be even more prudent to solicit references that have not been provided by the agency. Often times references given can be those of well-screened satisfied clients. You can bet that you will never be given "dissatisfied" clients to contact! The good news is that there are many good and honest adoption agencies available to you. The bad news is that you may not know until it is too late if you have chosen a disreputable agency. Be an educated consumer: research, research, research!

Part of your research must include finding out what the adoption agency fees are and if there are any additional (sometimes called "hidden") fees that may have to be paid at a later date. There are many families that are surprised by unexpected additional fees late in their adoption process. By this time, emotions are well into play, so many simply give in. Often these fees can range into the thousands of dollars. Be sure that you get a list of fees in writing, or better yet, have it included in your agency contract. Be sure to read, re-read and understand your contract prior to signing. Do not be afraid to ask questions about any part of your contract. As the saying goes, "better safe than sorry."

Generally speaking, adoption through an agency tends to be expensive. It is not at all unusual to see total adoption costs as much as $25,000 and upwards of $40,000 for an agency-assisted adoption. This high price tag makes it difficult or impossible for many families who wish to adopt to reach their goal. The alternative is independent adoption.

Independent Adoption

When a family chooses to adopt without the assistance of an adoption agency they are said to be adopting independently. "Independent adoption" is not a legal term. Those who adopt independently have to complete the exact same paperwork and go through the same procedures as with an agency adoption. The difference is that the family is on its own when it comes to finding and hiring translators, notaries, drivers and others. Fortunately, there are independent adoption professionals available to help complete the process. These independent adoption professionals are sometimes called "facilitators." Facilitators may be individuals with no special expertise who work under the "umbrella" of an in-country adoption agency or they may be highly educated and skilled individuals like attorneys who specialize in adoption law. You must be as careful in researching independent adoption facilitators and attorneys as you would be with adoption agencies.

Some may consider independent adoption as riskier than an agency assisted adoption. This is not necessarily true at all, and the savings of an independent adoption can be many thousands of dollars. With an independent adoption the family has much more control over the pace of preparation and the timing of the process. Most importantly, adopting independently allows many who could not afford to adopt the opportunity to realize their dream of adding a child to their family.

Going independent requires a little more of an adventurous spirit and some self-confidence. It may not be for everyone. The risks involved with independent adoption are no different than that of agency assisted adoption. Educating yourself about the adoption process and the thoroughly researching your options is the best plan of attack.

Chapter Two

What To Expect In Russia

Russia is a country that is rich in history, culture and tradition. *Russia is an enormous country, covering 6,592,850 sq. miles. Russia ranks 7th in world population with the 2001 population estimate being 145,471,000. Ethnic composition of Russia: Russian - 81.5%; Tatar - 3.8%; Ukrainian - 3.0%; Chuvash - 1.2%; Bashkir - 0.9%; Byelorussian - 0.8%; Moldovan - 0.7%; other - 8.1%. Primary Religions: Russian Orthodox, Islam, Judaism, Roman Catholicism, Protestant and Buddhism. Currency is the Ruble.

*Sources: Europa World Year Book; The World Factbook; World Population Prospects

Climate

The climate of Russia varies dramatically across the country, with the central regions experiencing a wide range of temperatures and heavy winter snows. The south is more temperate, with average temperatures ranging from 23 F in the winter to 74 F in the summer. Siberia and the north experience extremely low temperatures in the winter, with short, hot summers, while the eastern part of the country suffers extreme temperatures as well as milder forms of the monsoons typical to other parts of Asia.

Celebrated Russian Holidays

Important Russian holidays for one to note are:

- ❏ January 1 ....(New Year's Day)
- ❏ January 2 ....(New Year)
- ❏ January 7 ....(Orthodox Christmas)
- ❏ February 23 ....(Armed Forces Day)
- ❏ March 8 ....(Women's Day)
- ❏ May 1 ....(International Labor Day)
- ❏ May 2 ....(Spring Day)
- ❏ May 9 ....(Victory Day)
- ❏ June 12 ....(Russian Independence Day)
- ❏ November 7 ....(Day of State Reconciliation)
- ❏ December 12 ....(Constitution Day)

Economic Climate

Since the collapse of the former Soviet Union, Russia as a whole continues to struggle economically. While some areas tend to thrive (mostly major metropolitan areas), many rural areas are impoverished. It is important to understand this when traveling in Russia. You will see vast differences in the costs of meals, hotels and transportation from region to region. Costs can also vary widely for services such as translation of documents and translators and drivers. It is always prudent to do your homework and research the region you will be traveling to prior to your trip or get the advice of your adoption professional. There are many great resources for this kind of information on the internet.

The Russian population can be divided into four groups describing economic class.

Classes	%	Number of People
Poor (the income level is lower than the cost of living)	40.1	57.8 mil.
Low income (within the cost of living)	20.1	28.9 mil.
Middle class	33.4	48 mil.
Wealthy (finances exceed the high income standards)	6.4	9.2 mil.

* The official Information of the All-Russian Living Standard Center.

According to the official information of the "All-Russian Living Standard Center" dated 2001, the following table reflects three economic categories of the Russian population by regions. The poverty level in Russia is numerically defined at 2.00. The numbers to the right of each region indicates either above or below the poverty level. The overall average for Russia is at 2.14.

Regions with average or above average income of the population:

1.	Moscow - Federal city	6.31
2.	Khanty-Mansi Autonomous Area	3.94
3.	Tyumen regions	3.64
4.	Yamal-Nenets Autonomous Area	3.05
5.	Krasnoyarsk Territory	2.54
6.	St. Petersburg—Federal city	2.38
7.	Samara regions	2.28
8.	Republic of Komi	2.25
9.	Kemerovo regions	2.15
10.	Tomsk regions	2.12
11.	Krasnodar Territory	2.11
12.	Lipetsk regions	2.11
13.	Republic of North Ossetia	2.06
14.	Perm regions	2.03

Regions with low average income of the population

15.	Republic of Tatarstan	1.96
16.	Irkutsk regions	1.96
17.	Republic of Bashkortostan	1.95
18.	Tambov regions	1.92
19.	Belgorod regions	1.91
20.	Khabarovsk Territory	1.89
21.	Smolensk regions	1.87
22.	Rostov regions	1.86
23.	Volgograd regions	1.86

24.	Yaroslavl regions	1.85
25.	Omsk regions	1.81
26.	Oryol regions	1.81
27.	Orenburg regions	1.77
28.	Murmansk regions	1.76
29.	Altai Territory	1.72
30.	Chelyabinsk regions	1.70
31.	Republic of Sakha (Yakutia)	1.69
32.	Moscow regions	1.69
33.	Taimyr Autonomous Area	1.68
34.	Nenets Autonomous Area	1.64
35.	Republic of Khakasia	1.63
36.	Tula regions	1.63
37.	Ryazan regions	1.60
38.	Udmurt Republic	1.60
39.	Sverdlovsk regions	1.58
40.	Kabardin-Balkar Republic	1.57
41.	Republic of Altai	1.57
42.	Novgorod regions	1.56
43.	Republic of Karelia	1.56
44.	Kursk regions	1.55
45.	Nizhny Novgorod regions	1.54
46.	Voronezh regions	1.53
47.	Astrakhan regions	1.53
48.	Stavropol Territory	1.53
49.	Kamchatka regions	1.53
50.	Amur regions	1.50
51.	Sakhalin regions	1.50
52.	Arkhangelsk regions	1.47
53.	Magadan regions	1.46
54.	Republic of Buryatia	1.45
55.	Evenk Autonomous Area	1.45
56.	Kaliningrad regions	1.42
57.	Chuvash Republic	1.37

58.	Ulyanovsk regions	1.35
59.	Saratov regions	1.35
60.	Pskov regions	1.35
61.	Tver regions	1.33
62.	Republic of Mordovia	1.31
63.	Penza regions	1.31
64.	Kaluga regions	1.30
65.	Bryansk regions	1.29
66.	Kurgan regions	1.29
67.	Kostroma regions	1.29
68.	Republic of Adygeya (Adygeya)	1.28
69.	Novosibirsk regions	1.27
70.	Chukchi Autonomous Area	1.25
71.	Republic of Dagestan	1.21
72.	Vologda regions	1.20
73.	Karachayevo-Cherkess Republic	1.20
74.	Primork Territory	1.18
75.	Vladimir regions	1.15
76.	Leningrad regions	1.10
77.	Republic of Kalmykia	1.08
78.	Republic of Tuva	1.07
79.	Ingush Republic	1.02
80.	Kirov regions	1.00

Regions with the poorest average income level of the population

81.	Chita regions	1.95
82.	Koryak Autonomous Area	0.87
83.	Komi-Permyak Autonomous Area	0.87
84.	Ivanovo regions	0.84
85.	Republic of Mari El,	0.81
86.	Aginsky Buryat Autonomous Area	0.79

87.	Ust-Ordynsky Buryat Autonomous Area	0.53
88.	Jewish Autonomous regions	n/a
89.	Chechen Republic	n/a

Since May 1, 2002 the minimum monthly wage has been set at 450 rubles, which is about $14 US (Federal Law of Russian Federation # 42-FL on April 29, 2002).

The official Poverty Guidelines during the fourth quarter of 2001 was 1575 rubles per month (about $50 US). The average monthly salary for the same period of time was approximately twice the poverty level at 3,393 rubles ($109 US). The average retirement payments were lower than the poverty level at 1,135 rubles (about $36 US).

Currency and Exchange

Currency exchange (Rubles to Dollars or Dollars to Rubles) can fluctuate from hour to hour, day to day and place to place. Be careful of the "Black Market" exchange. It is best to deal with legal exchange establishments.

While hotel, airport and train station establishments give the worst exchange rates, you might try various other places such as banks, exchange shops along a main street, etc. There can be quite a difference in rates from one shop to another.

Be careful of asking an individual (such as an escort or facilitator) to do your exchanging for you. Some are notorious for taking advantage of foreign citizens, even pocketing as much as 30% of the transaction. Remember, it is your money.

It is recommended that you bring new $20, $50, and $100 bills that are crisp, clean and un-creased condition and unmarked by ink or stamping. Marked or older bills can bring lower exchange rates or may not be accepted at all. Traveler's checks are accepted at most exchange facilities and are the same rate of exchange as the Dollar, but beware, some establishments take a small percentage for exchanging them.

Many hotels, airlines, trains and some restaurants accept credit cards. This is more likely in the larger cities than other areas. There are limited ATM services in Russia; they also come with a "fee" for the service.

Culture Shock

Travel to Russia can be quite a difficult experience for the first-timer. You should prepare yourself for some frustration and inconvenience. The best rule about traveling in Russia is "expect the unexpected".

Many unprepared travelers cannot get over the inconveniences they experience. Seasoned travelers, especially those who have been to regions of the planet that are not as technologically advanced as the United States, know that a flexible and relaxed frame of mind is the best antidote when traveling. Many even allow themselves to enjoy the experience and value the opportunity to live for a short period of time in a manner that is totally different from what they are used to. This ranges from things such as "pollution and air quality" to "toilet facilities and amenities" to "size of paper napkins in a restaurant" (or lack thereof). The more rural you get with your adoption visit and tour, the wider the gap from the "normal."

Some of my clients have had opportunity to experience the old fashioned "outhouse". Of course, this was not at any of the hotels used. A good traveler will always prepare for the "unknown" without overdoing it. While most of us can put up with these little inconveniences and differences, do not overlook the opportunity to visit and absorb a part of the world that, only a few years ago, was inaccessible by most foreigners. You are adding an entirely new dimension to your adoption experience. Culture!

Technology

Available technology in Russia can be anything from State-of-the-art to antique. As with many things, international communication, either through the internet or telephone service, can be frustrating at times. While in more modern facilities, and within larger cities and hotels, you will find more reliable equipment. Rural areas or smaller or more remote cities may use telephone equipment that is much more antiquated by US standards.

You may find, when calling from many Russian telephones, the connection seems to gradually deteriorate as you are talking. This is sometimes remedied by banging the receiver against a desk or wall. An unconventional short fix, but it works! Disconnections and bad connections are frequent and should be expected.

Phone cards can be purchased at various places such as the Subway stations, some Post Offices and most convenience stores. Keep in mind that in some hotels, especially the more expensive hotels in Moscow and St. Petersburg, a call to the US can cost as much as $15 per minute.

Pay phones are not as readily available in Russia as they are in other countries. When you do find one, it may not work, even in the larger cities. Be sure you tell your loved ones at home that you will try to call or e-mail them, but if they do not hear from you for a day or two, they should not panic. Most cities have "Internet Cafes," some of which operate 24 hours a day. This is generally a very inexpensive way to communicate back home. The costs for this service can range from a half-dollar to about four dollars per hour.

Computers and e-mail do work, but at slower modem speeds. There is no high-speed internet access yet. Do not expect to find computer ports in a hotel room unless you are staying in Moscow or St. Petersburg in a luxury hotel. If you do have internet access from your hotel room you can purchase increments of time for access.

Packing for Russia

How you pack for Russia will depend on who and how many are traveling. You will pack much differently for one person than you will for two adults and a child or children. The best advice is to pack light! Pack only things you KNOW you will need and then if you have additional space (and you do not mind the heavier load) you can add what might be on your "B" list. The reason for taking less is that it is not easy going through the streets, airports and train stations lugging multiple full suitcases. Even if the suitcases are on wheels, you should not assume the sidewalks and building entrances are accommodating. Sidewalks contain many potholes, construction areas and uneven patch jobs while many buildings are built with endless steps (not handicap friendly as in other countries). Baggage weight is strictly enforced (check with the airlines) and for each additional kilogram overweight, there is a surcharge. So the moral here is "lighter is better".

Below is a list of some additional items (other than the obvious) that you may wish to consider bringing along with you if they apply.

- **Voltage converter (for Eastern Europe)**

- **Antiseptic wet wipes**

- **Tissues**

- **Necessary prescription medication** (if needed and also a copy of your prescription)

- **"Backup" Eyewear** (glasses/contacts – if a concern)

- **Shower shoes/slippers**

- **Laundry Detergent** (small amount)

- **Shampoo and soap** (you will find only tiny amounts or none at all in many hotels)

- **Camera** (film readily available in Russia)

- **A few plastic (disposable) grocery bags** (these are not usually given in Russia with purchases. You must pay extra for bags "if" you can get them)

- **Gifts/Souvenirs** (if you wish to bring something – think "lightweight")

- **Small notebook and pencil/pen** (for making notes)

- **Russian/English dictionary or electronic translator**

- **Small amount of snacks** (for those times you get hungry and nothing is open).

- **"Busy" items** (if traveling with children)

- **Head Lice treatment** (if you are traveling to get your child, this is a very common problem among orphans. Not recommended for infants)

- **Laptop computer** (ONLY if you "have to have it")

Items that I would recommend you NOT take along are valuables such as expensive jewelry. Wedding bands and non-extravagant jewelry are fine and do not attract attention.

Dress

To travelers, especially from the United States, you will most certainly notice a pride in the way Russian citizens dress. You will not see very many people in "relaxed wear" like tennis shoes, jeans or cult fashion as with the younger generation in the US.

Even with everyday wear, most Russians take great pride in their appearances. You will notice that the men wear sports jackets or suit jackets (except in harsh temperatures), nice slacks and leather shoes. The women will wear dresses (slacks in harsher temperatures), high heels, their hair stylishly cut and in place, and of course, makeup. Even the children are dressed with great pride and fashion sense.

If you pay attention, you will even see that most teenagers and children going out with their friends and family are "dressed up." If you do not want to stand out in the crowd, you may want to consider your fashion options.

Most Russians wear darker fashions, black or gray. Accessories such as shoes, belts and purses are typically black leather. You can expect to do more walking than you are probably used to. You may want to consider comfortable shoes. These should be black because lighter colored shoes will probably not stay clean for more than a few minutes.

Always dress appropriately for your Court appearance. A suit or coat and tie for men, dress or pant suit for women is highly recommended. This is NOT the place to look casual.

If you will be traveling during the harsher winter months, you should prepare yourself accordingly. Be sure that your winter wear is designed and manufactured for harsh winter conditions; this includes coats, undergarments (silk thermals are nice) and boots/shoes. Ski type apparel is not seen often in Russia as a way to dress for warmth. Winter coats are of the "dress" variety, and are usually manufactured for the bitterly cold and often windy weather.

Dining

Dining in Russia can be a wonderful culinary experience in the right places. Food is usually prepared fresh and with great care. You are encouraged to explore new and delicious foods while you are in Russia.

American style fast food is almost non-existent except in major cities. You will find convenient "deli-style" stores with a variety of meat products similar to salami or other smoked or prepared meat, fresh or prepared fish such as pickled herring, lox or smoked salmon, fresh baked breads and rolls and other bakery treats. Most of these places also carry a variety of beverages from water and soda to traditional drinks such as Kvas and a wide assortment of beers, wines and cognacs as well as the traditional vodka (and so many brands to choose from for the vodka connoisseur).

As you would in most foreign countries, you are advised to drink water from a bottled source. If you have a sensitive stomach, you may wish to bring your favorite over-the-counter medicines to help in case of an unexpected food reaction.

Coffee lovers may suffer some withdrawals since the coffee in Russia is typically instant coffee or something similar to espresso. If you don't take sugar, be sure to tell your hostess, it is usually added for you.

You will not find the tables in many restaurants adorned with bottles of ketchup, mustard, sugar, cream, etc. These items are usually offered at an extra cost. The cost of food and drink in Russia (outside of the fancy metropolitan restaurants) is usually extremely reasonable, if not downright cheap for what you get, so don't be afraid to order what you want. You won't have to take out a loan to pay the tab.

Note: There are many quality restaurants in the major cities such as Moscow and St. Petersburg. These will offer fine dining with what you would expect from a quality establishment, but be prepared to pay prices similar to those in the US for the same service. Tipping is not common in Russia. Most expensive restaurants however do expect tips.

Getting Around

You will probably arrive in Moscow (or depart from there) and then travel on to the regions you have chosen for your adoption. Because things in Russia are typically not without glitches, it is a very good idea to plan to spend some extra time in the country. Traveling to Russia with small children on the first trip is not recommended, especially for inexperienced travelers. The trip can be especially difficult for young children, and your attention will need to be focused on the completion of your adoption process. You will find that your days are sometimes very stressful and comprised of a grueling schedule. Because of jet lag, your sleep patterns will be disrupted, and fatigue will set in very easily. You will not find it easy to just to head back to the hotel for a quick nap or to stop somewhere for a quick bite to eat. Children will feel these effects more intensely than adults.

Traveling inside Russia is much different than that of traveling within the US. Airports and terminals are often small and lack many of the conveniences of US airports. Trains are a very common means of transportation for most Russians and foreign visitors. These range from very nice modern trains to very old, but still serviceable trains.

Transportation within most areas of Russia is more reasonable in cost than that in the US. However, in the major cities you will find transportation costs fairly expensive. Taxi service in the major cities like Moscow can be very expensive. You probably will be bombarded with "available" taxi drivers as you exit most airports. Be careful, and negotiate your price before you accept a driver. Many will even tell you it is inexpensive and yet charge you many times the going rate. Better yet, if you can arrange service prior to arrival you can save quite a bit. Just be sure to understand and agree to the cost before you ride. Tipping a driver is not necessary since the tip is usually included.

When you travel to some of the outer regions of Russia, the lack of air transportation may require you to return to Moscow in order to connect to another region. First time travelers will often look at a map and see two cities that appear relatively close together, but in reality they can be a day or more apart to travel. It is a good idea to check schedules carefully when traveling to outer destinations. Flights may be available only once per week in some regions. There are some regional capitals that do not have airports or connections to Moscow, for example Birobidzhan. Plan your travel in country carefully.

Remember as you travel through Russia: delays are common conveniences almost non-existent and things may seem quite disorganized and confusing. Many things may not make any sense at all, but it is the system in which you will have to work if adopting from Russia. Expect the unexpected and you will do just fine. Russia can be especially frustrating to those that are very organized and expect others to be the same. Good advice: Relax and be flexible!

Hotels

There are approximately 2500 hotels in the Russian Federation, of which about 150 specialize in accommodating foreign guests. Some hotels meet international standards, whereas others are very basic.

Although prices can vary widely, most hotels are reasonable, especially outside of Moscow and St. Petersburg. They also range from the very basic (a tiny room with a tiny bed and very limited bathroom comforts) to the somewhat comfortable, comparable to mid range quality hotels in the US. Obviously, from town to town and place to place, there will be varying degrees of quality and comfort.

For example, some hotels have specific times for hot water use. You may find that the hot water is turned on only during a specified period of the day. If traveling in the summer, do not expect air conditioning in most hotels. It generally does not exist. If you open your windows for fresh air, be prepared for the ever-pesky mosquito.

Since many of the more modest hotels have very small rooms, you may wish to take this into consideration especially if traveling with your children. Do not expect king or queen sizes in most hotels. Generally only twin size beds are available. You can always ask for more bedding if a child should have to sleep on a floor. Again, this can be, and usually is, an extra charge.

Shopping and Sightseeing

Touring and sightseeing is a favorite pastime of Russian citizens, especially during the summer months. As you travel through Russia and do your own sightseeing you will quickly notice, however, that there are two sets of prices given in some tourist attractions and hotels, one for citizens and one for foreigners. It is not unusual to see the price of an entrance ticket to a museum or other attraction as much as ten times more for a foreigner. Grin and bear it. This is perfectly legal in Russia.

If you are shopping in the open-air marketplaces or among the multitude of street vendors of Russia, it is customary to barter. Do not accept the first price given (unless you already know the items value). Usually, the first price is an inflated price (primarily for foreigners). This is especially true for the prices of souvenirs and crafts. If the vendor does not accept your "fair" price, there will be others that will. You always have the option to go back if you feel you must have this item. If you have a Russian friend, it is always helpful to let him or her make the approach and do the "dealing" for you. They usually know the game (and the value of an item) well.

Another thing you should keep in mind is that what may be "reasonable" to you in terms of cost may be actually far too much to pay. Remember, the state of the economy in Russia is very different than in the United States. Goods and services tend to be much less expensive (except in the largest cities) and paying high prices actually inflates the prices for others that will shop after you. There is no good reason to spend more than you have to.

Russia is a great place to shop for any items that you intend to donate to the orphanage or give as gifts to helpers along the way. If you wish to give something, you should consider purchasing items in country rather than lugging things from America or another country. You can find quality goods that are happily accepted by any orphanage or individual.

When trying to speak to Russians, you will find that most do not know English, or they know very little as compared to other European countries. You should take the time to learn a few key words or phrases (examples provided in the back of this book). This will help you feel more comfortable and the person you are communicating with will appreciate it. Of course, it will also help with your future children!

Take Advantage

Once at your regional destination, do not overlook trying the local fare. Food and drink can be as diverse as in any other country. You will notice many similarities, but each region boasts its own variety and style, just as each city highlights its own history. Do try and take the time to find out about local events.

During the mild days of summer, there tends to be much more to see and do, especially outdoors. Bazaars, celebrations and special events are popular in most regions during the summer.

Russia has so much to offer. If you get to know the history, culture and the people, and you keep an open and flexible mind, you may find the urge, as many do, to return. Maybe you will even want to further expand your family.

Russian People

Do not forget about the Russian people themselves. Because Russia is so rich in history and culture, you will find a people that are both proud and protective of their country.

Russian people, by in large, have an "image" of foreigners, especially those from America, that has been hewn out of the last century of communistic rule and spoon-fed propaganda. Perhaps it is not much different than a foreigner's conjured and inaccurate images of Russians. In the last decade, due to the increasingly close relationship between Russia and the rest of the world, a flood of information has filtered into Russia about the west. Much of this information meets with not only curiosity, but also skepticism and a certain amount of scrutiny. Not surprisingly, the greatest image perceived of the west is that of a people ruled by materialism.

Russians are a people that project modest means. Russian people can be very patient as they observe foreigners in order to form their own opinion. There will naturally be a bit of nervousness until trust can be developed. The best way to interact with the people of Russia is with respect. You will find that getting upset or threatening will not intimidate someone into doing anything better or faster for you, and neither will begging or pleading. Intellect and respect will prevail.

If you visit the home of a Russian and compliment the owner on a particular item you see, it may be handed to you as a gift. This is not uncommon. The hospitality of Russians is such that they will give you their last piece of bread to make you feel welcome in their home. They would think nothing of missing the next day's food as the sacrifice for this event.

The Darker Side of Russia

There is a disturbing side of Russia, however. The existence of criminals often referred to as "mafia" or the "underground" is all too real, and they have a negative effect on many parts of the economy. The break up of the former Soviet Union resulted in a new element of "entrepreneurs." These shadowy characters tend to have their hands in just about every kind of business activity throughout the country, adoption not excluded, with their hands held out for "their share" of the profits. Many things do not get done in much of Russia without taking care of this element.

Don't be frightened. You will probably never see this side of things, since it is usually handled behind the scenes. Some regions try hard to discourage this type of criminal activity, but it can be found almost everywhere, including among those working in an official capacity. Of course, not all are this way, but do not be surprised when you see the signs. There are ways to avoid much of this if you are well represented.

Chapter Three

About The Children

Although there are many similarities in the orphaned children from region to region in Russia, the vastness alone can create differences in everything from ethnicity to quality of care and more. It might be helpful to understand some of the realities of the children, their care and their environment. Again, it is not possible to provide every detail and accuracy about every orphan and orphanage, but this chapter should provide an accurate overview and some additional insight.

Types of State Facilities for Children

Dom Rebenka

A Dom Rebenka is a public health institution designed for bringing up and rendering medical care to orphan children, children whose parents are not in the position to take care of them, and children with physical or mental needs. In a Dom

Rebenka, children from birth up to three years of age and children with physical and mental concerns up to four years of age are raised. Children arrive at the Dom Rebenka from maternity homes, hospitals, and from families. In Russia there are about 422 Doms Rebenka.

The major activity of an infant home is caring for children and rendering medical and health services. Children who are kept in a Dom Rebenka are provided with room and board, clothes, footwear, furniture, and toys according to the established norms.

A child may be discharged from a Dom Rebenka when they are taken back by their families, transferred to educational children's homes (boarding schools related to organizations of social welfare), or placed for adoption or under guardianship (similar to foster care) with families.

Detski Dom

A Detski Dom is a State educational institution where children from 3 to 16 years of age (in some cases 18) who have been left without parental custody (due to their parents' death, removal of their parental rights, taking children away under the established procedure, and other reasons, and also the children whose parents have difficulties in maintaining and taking care of them), are kept, educated and brought up. There are Detski Doms for children of preschool age (3-7 years of age), school age (7-18 years of age), and those with all ages.

There are more than 820 Detski Doms in Russia. Children are admitted to a Detski Dom under a variety of circumstances ranging from referrals from infant homes to placement by parents and relatives who are unable to take proper care of the child.

The main objective of the children's home is to provide proper conditions for the upbringing and education of children. The administrators, teachers and other workers in the home assist the children in a choice of a future profession, as well as prepare them for independent life and labor. They are provided with board, clothes, footwear, games, toys and school supplies according to the established norms.

Shkola-Internat

A Shkola-Internat is a State institution (boarding school) that provides for the maintenance, education, development and upbringing of orphan children of school age, as well as for children who experience problems with their development or education.

There are several types of Shkolas-Internat: Those with a general educational program for children who do not have serious personal development problems; supplementary Shkolas-Internat for children with oligophrenia (mental retardation) of a mild degree and mental and speech delays and Shkolas-Internat for children with deeper defects that are under the supervision of the Ministry of Social Protection. All three of these Shkolas-Internat fall under the supervision of the Ministry of Education of The Russian Federation.

In recent years Shkolas-Internats appeared for talented children who have been left without parental custody. Presently there are more than 150 comprehensive Shkolas-Internat for orphan children and children who have been left without parental custody, and 178 Shkolas-Internat for orphan children with physical and mental needs.

Priut

A Priut (pree-oot) is a special State institution related to institutions of social protection of population, a new form of assistance to orphan children and children who are in difficult situations. Priuts are sometimes formed by public organizations. A Priut is an institution of temporary stay for children.

The main tasks of the Priut employees include rendering psychological and pedagogical support of the child. The main goal of this type of Priut is the diagnosis of the existent situation of the child and the determination of his (her) further destiny. The Bodies of Trusteeship, social workers and Shkola-Internat specialists most often place children in such a Priut. Today in Russia there are more than 300 Priuts.

Centers of Temporary Custody

A Center of Temporary Custody is a temporary placement of the child for the purpose of providing urgent special help. This help is necessary when the child is urgently taken away from the family, and when there is the need to organize urgent psychological, pedagogical or social support.

An important part of the work of these centers is the organization of correctional and rehabilitation activities. Most often the Bodies of Social Protection of Population and Public Organizations form such centers. Today in Russia there are about

150 social and rehabilitation centers to children who have been left without parental custody, and centers of temporary stay for orphan children.

The Truth About Most Orphans

The problem of children's orphanages remains one of the more vexed and insoluble problems within Russia. First of all, owing to the inability of the Russian authorities to reform the antihuman, inefficient, wasteful, and sometimes harmful conditions of orphanages, all the governmental programs and all the enormous expenditures continue to produce an even worse environment for the children who have been left without parental custody.

The total number of orphan children and children who have been left without parental custody has grown by almost double during the last 10 years, and at the same time the children's population of Russia has been reduced to a little over 6 million. Orphan children and children who have been left without parental custody constituted 1 % of the children's population in 1991 and almost 2 % in 2000.

The rate that orphan children are placed in families has remained at the same level for the last 10 years. Then and now 27 %-28 % of orphan children are placed in orphan's homes (the rest presumably are taken in by relatives). At the same time the number of children taken away from parents grows every year. Between 1993 and 1999 the rate that children are removed from family homes in relation to the children's population has grown 2 to 1 (from 25,896 up to 50,018 in total).

This chart shows the number of new children without parental custody for the respective years. It is estimated that from 2000 to 2002 the number has remained nearly constant, resulting in over 123,000 new children admitted to the orphanages each year.

1992	1995	1996	1997	1998	1999	2000
67286	113296	103243	105534	110930	113913	123204

* Statistics From the State report. "About the position of children in the Russian Federation"

In Russia there is no alternative to the social orphanage system, like the foster care system in the United States.

Children Without Parental Custody are "Second-Rate Citizens"

According to the data of human rights organizations, all children left in the care of the Russian government immediately become the victims of a deeply ingrained prejudice: that all children abandoned by their parents have some defect. One of the sources of such prejudice is the common occurrence of mothers leaving babies with serious defects in the maternity hospital. Parents often act that way under pressure from medical workers, who scare them into believing that everyone will turn away from the family raising a disabled child.

The prejudice also covers the children who do not seem to have serious physical or mental defects but who were born into families with serious social, financial and medical problems, including alcoholism.

The fear that the child will be some kind of "defective product" is based upon the fact that doctors advise mothers whose children have mental or physical defects to put them to a children's home and "to try again." Accordingly, healthy children, abandoned because of the difficult financial condition of parents or unfavorable home conditions, are unfairly marked as "defective."

As a result these abandoned children are doomed to the status of "orphans." In their medical cards they have records of physical and psychological "risk factors" related to their origin. Evidence collected by human rights organizations has been corroborated by the data of the research conducted by the Swiss experts from the International Committee for Child Dignity (C.I.D.E) and published in 1995. The C.I.D.E. researchers have found out that though the Russian specialists follow strict criteria of psychological diagnostics, they also make records of such information in the medical card of a child. In the West this would be considered only as potential risk factors, while in Russia, with regard to an orphan child, the same information is taken as evidence of the inherent defects. Under the data of the C.I.D.E. report, the above mentioned applies to the following children:

❏ Children born to alcohol addicts, or children whose mothers suffered from depression during pregnancy, are diagnosed of "encephalopathy" and remain with it up to legal age;

❏ orphan children are diagnosed as mentally retarded;

❏ in the opinion of Russian doctors, children with a single physical defect (for example, cleft lip or speech defect), are not quite normal.

The International Legislation on Human Rights prohibits discrimination on a number of grounds, including the factors of "birth or other circumstance". According to the United Nations, principles of protecting individuals with mental disorders and improving the psychiatric aid, "the basis for diagnosing mental disorder shall never be the political, economic or social status or culture, race or religion affiliation or any other cause which is not directly related to the state of mental health."

In practice, the Russian system ignores this principle, as well as the fundamental provisions of the International Covenant on Economic, Social and Cultural rights, considering children from the families with low social and economic status and children with genetic defects as a special class. The Russian system attributes to such children the inherent tendency to antisocial conduct, which is supposedly rooted in their origin. The system brands them for life and officially restricts their participation in the life of Russian society. Children left without parental custody and diagnosed with "oligophrenia," (i.e. mental retardation) will have this recorded in their medical documents, moving from one institution to another. These children do not have any opportunity to have the diagnosis revised or disaffirmed. Even technical school graduates who have the diagnosis of "a mild degree of oligophrenia," faced great difficulties when asking to remove these diagnoses from their medical documents.

The number of these children grows every year. Children left since birth without parental custody often have physical and developmental delays as compared with children of the same age raised in families. One of the reasons for these delays is the considerable lack of attention to the mental development of such children in the crucial period of infancy, while they are kept at state children's homes. The orphan child has nobody to work in his behalf to dispute the unfavorable conclusion of the medical and pedagogical authorities. The diagnosis of "a severe degree of oligophrenia" made by the authorities means greater likelihood of premature death for an orphan child at a Psychoneurological Closed Internat, which often resembles a warehouse instead of a children's institution.

A child with the diagnosis of "a severe degree of oligophrenia," (severe mental retardation) is directed to a closed institution. There, children for all practical purposes do not receive any education and have minimal care. Children are kept at these institutions up to the age of 18 and then they are transferred to the same kinds of institutions for adults. Despite the fact that independent Russian experts on problems of childhood express negative opinions about these institutions (specifically that that the children's death rate in these institutions is twice that of the death rate of similar children being raised in families), these institutions flourish.

Children who do not have any serious medical conditions and who are pronounced fit for training have more luck. They are directed to orphanages.

Children without parental custody, inmates of state facilities, belong to one of the least protected categories of the population of Russia. After leaving the care of the state orphanage system, 30 % of the children become vagrants, 20 % become criminals and 10 % commit suicide. Only 40% go on to live some kind of "normal" life.

* Statistics From the State report. "About the position of children in the Russian Federation"

Children with Disabilities

The condition of disabled children in state orphan institutions (Closed Internats) is disastrous. It is a sad fact that these children do not have proper medical care. Because Closed Internats do not fall under the institutions of public health, they lack the necessary medical personnel, remedies and facilities. These children do not get necessary surgical corrections of inherent defects of the skeletal system and vital internal organs. Deceased children do not undergo autopsies.

Closed Internats are really not much more than children's concentration camps, where disabled children are held without any prospect of improving their health, development and adjustment. Disabled children placed in a Closed Internat are legally dispossessed of their rights to living quarters outside of the orphanage. This fact is likely due to the fact that most of these children die after leaving the care of the orphanage and, therefore, do not claim the former living quarters.

When parents place their child in an institution, the child's registration is reserved, and it reserves the right to housing. However, parents who do not take the child back from the institution may use the privileges granted to the disabled children and receive additional living quarters from the state.

When they turn 16 (in some cases 18) children are released from the Closed Internat. In fact, none of the children who have survived are taken back by parents or relatives, and all of them are transferred to special institutions for adults. Under the procedure in force, their names are removed from the lists of tenants of their homes and they are registered at this institution. Disabled children are made to sign the appropriate papers, and usually they do not realize what documents they have signed (as the disabled children are not taught anything systematically at Closed Internats. They have no experience in handling documents and they do not understand what these documents mean).

* From the independent report of the Russian public organizations at a special session of the General Assembly of the United Nations, New York, September 19-20, 2001

The Allowances

(Clothing and Goods Rationing)

You might be interested in what the Government provides to the children in these orphanages. The list below states what new items are given to the children in a typical year. In reality, many children get hand-me-downs, items that do not fit or just they do not receive some of these listed items at all. It is very interesting to ask an orphan or former orphan to go through this list and hear their comments.

The allowances for providing the foster-children of children's homes, orphan children and children without parental custody with clothes, footwear and soft stock at comprehensive Internats of all types, institutions of the social protection of population as well as the preschool foster-children at boarding schools are as follows:

(Approved by the Governmental Regulation of the Russian Federation of May 14, 2001 # 374)

The description of clothes, footwear and soft stock	Units	Per one foster-child of school age		Per one foster-child of preschool age	
		Number	Term of wear, service (years)	Number	Term of wear, service (years)
Clothing					
Winter coat, fur-coat	Pieces	1	2	1	2
Spring/autumn coat, jacket	-«-	1	2	1	2
Woolen school suit for a boy	-«-	1	2	-	-
Woolen two-piece school suit for a girl	-«-	1	2	-	-
White cotton school shirt for a boy	-«-	2	1	-	-
Sport suit and gumshoes	Sets	2	2	-	-
Summer suit and woolen suit for a boy	-«-	2	2	4	2
Dress (skirt, blouse)	Pieces	4	2	4	2
Home dressing gown for a girl	-«-	2	1	2	1
Shirt for a boy	-«-	4	1	4	1
Dressy woolen suit for a boy	Sets	1	2	1	1
Dressy summer suit for a boy	-«-	1	2	1	1
Woolen sweater (pullover)	Pieces	2	1	1	1
Dressy summer dress	-«-	1	2	1	2
Hose for a girl	-«-	2	1	2	1
Summer headgear	-«-	1	1	1	1
Waist-belt for a boy	-«-	1	1	1	2
Half-woolen scarf	-«-	1	2	1	2

The description of clothes, footwear and soft stock	Units	Per one foster-child of school age		Per one foster-child of preschool age	
		Number	Term of wear, service (years)	Number	Term of wear, service (years)
Clothing					
Gloves (mittens)	Pairs	2	1	2	1
Bra	Pieces	4	1	-	-
Knickers	-«-	5	1	5	1
Sport shorts	-«-	2	1	3	1
Shorts	-«-	2	1	2	1
Sleeveless undershirt	-«-	3	1	3	1
Sports shirt	-«-	2	1	2	1
Cotton socks, half hose	Pairs	10	1	6	1
Shoes (sandals, sneakers)	-«-	3	1	3	1
Slippers	-«-	2	1	2	1
Felt boots (winter footwear)	-«-	2	1	2	1
Gum-boots	-«-	1	2	1	2
Skiing suit	Pieces	1	2	1	2
Sport cap	-«-	1	2	1	2
Nightgowns, pajamas	-«-	2	1	3	1
Tights	-«-	10	1	10	1
Dress for a sand-box, bathing suit, trunks	-«	1	1	2	1
Rubber cap	-«-	1	2	1	2
Working wear	Sets	1	2	-	-
Briefcase, bag	Pieces	2	2	-	-
Suitcase	-«-	1	5	1	5
Pinafore, bib for a preschool child	-«-	-	-	2	1

The description of clothes, footwear and soft stock	Units	Per one foster-child of school age		Per one foster-child of preschool age	
		Number	Term of wear, service (years)	Number	Term of wear, service (years)
Soft stock					
Bed sheets	Pieces	3	2	6	2
Blanket cover	-«-	2	2	4	2
Under pillow-case	-«	1	4	1	4
Upper pillow-case	-«-	3	2	6	2
Towel	Pieces	4	2	4	2
Terry towel	-«-	3	3	3	2
Woolen blanket or quilt	-«-	2	5	2	5
Cotton blanket	-«	1	5	1	5
Mattress	-«-	1	6	1	4
Coverlet	-«-	1	5	1	5
Pillow	-«-	1	4	1	4
Bed-side rug	-«-	1	5	1	5

Chapter Four

The Adoption Process

This chapter contains detailed explanations of the various parts of the process that must be followed to complete a Russian adoption.

INS

Once you have decided that an international adoption is right for you and your family, you should immediately submit an I-600A (Application for Advance Processing of Orphan Petition) to your local Immigration and Naturalization Service (INS) office. You can order this form by calling 800-870-3676 or at the INS web site: *http://www.ins.usdoj.gov*

The I-600A is your request to the United States Department of Immigration to approve you for foreign adoption in advance of selecting a child. Complete this form, signed by both spouses (unless single parent) and send to your local INS office along with a $460 money order for the processing fee. You will also need to submit $50 for each prospective adoptive parent and for each adult member (18 years of age or older) of the household for a fingerprint fee. Each INS office currently operates somewhat independently so approval time frames and processing can very from state to state.

Since the processing of your application can take several months, you should begin this step even if your homestudy is not complete and even if you have not decided on a foreign country from which to adopt.

Once your homestudy is completed, your homestudy agency will submit it to the INS. Upon completion (concluding you are indeed eligible to adopt), the INS will send you an approval form, the I-171H (Notice of Favorable Determination Concerning Application for Advance Processing of Orphan Petition). You will use this form to prove to the adoption court that you have INS approval to adopt. The INS approval process can take time. It's not unusual to wait between 1 to 4 months or more for your approval to arrive. At the time you receive your approval, the INS will send a cable notice to the US Embassy in Russia. You will need to contact the Embassy to make sure that they received the INS cable (this can be done by e-mail, fax or phone).

Homestudy

Select a licensed homestudy agency in your state who will work with you to prepare the homestudy documents and the INS I-600A. Homestudy agencies pricing and processing times can vary. You should check with Social Services organizations within your state, local government, church or your community or you can try this sources web site for qualified homestudy agencies at: *http://www.1-800-homestudy.com*

A social worker from your homestudy agency will visit your home to discuss your reasons for adoption. He/she will evaluate your family, lifestyle and finances among other things. It can take from approximately 3 weeks to 8 weeks for your social worker to complete this process. The homestudy guidelines must follow the requirements of your state, the INS and the Russian Government. It is important to prepare a comprehensive homestudy. Most social workers or homestudy agencies that work with international adoption know what exactly what is required.

By Russian Law, all homestudies are valid for one year and must be updated after this expiration date. It should also be updated should you have any major changes or if you have relocated during your processing.

Collecting Documents

You must assemble a number of documents (your dossier) in order to complete your application as prospective adoptive parents. For most Russian regions you will need two sets of documents, one for the Regional or Federal Operator of the Databank of Children Without Parental Custody (formerly known as the Department of Education [DoE] or the Ministry of Education [MoE]) and the other for the Regional Court. You must have each document properly completed, notarized and Apostilled (see sections on Notarization of Documents and Apostille later in this book).

Translation of Documents

Once you have collected all of your documents and had them notarized and Apostilled, your documents must then be translated into Russian. Translations must be certified by a Notary in the Consulate of the Russian Federation in the USA or by a Notary Public in the territory of the Russian Federation. Each document should be carefully reviewed before submitting them to the proper Russian authorities. Russia continues to be very suspicious with any documents so the process can be interrupted and even jeopardized with even an innocent mistake such as a typographical error. I cannot emphasize enough to cross every "t" and dot every "i" and double-check this again and again for consistency throughout before you finalize your documents prior to translation.

Obtaining Your Passports

You should apply for your US Passports immediately if you have not already done so by this time. Your passports must be issued prior to the application for a Russian Visa. This takes time as well so it is better to take care of this early.

Submitting Documents to the Russian Government

Once you have completed all of your required documents for the Regional/Federal Operator of the Databank of Children Without Parental Custody and have had them translated and notarized, it is now time to submit them. They can be submitted by you or by your agency's representative. After the appropriate Russian authorities approve your dossier they will place your personal information into the databank. You will then wait to be notified that you can travel to obtain information about the child/ren meeting your description that are available for adoption. The time frame in obtaining a referral can vary greatly depending on many factors such as age/sex/health of the child you would like as well as the number of children you wish to adopt. If you submitted documents in person to the Regional/Federal Operator of the Databank of Children Without Parental Custody, they are obligated to provide confidential information about available children for adoption by foreign people within 10 days of receiving your application (Articles 10,11,12 of the Federal Law of the State Databank of Children Without Parental Custody).

Russian Visa

In order to enter Russia, you will need to obtain a Russian Visa. There are a number of types of Visa's such as business, tourist, single-entry, double-entry and even a multiple entry. In most cases, it is better to apply for a double entry Visa that is good for three months from the issue date. This should be enough time to travel for your second trip and complete your adoption.

There are a number of travel agencies that will provide you with Russian Visa service either as a stand-alone or coupled with your travel.

Travel to get the Referral and meet a Child

As soon as you receive the invitation to travel, you may make your plans to travel to the appropriate region and obtain your referral from the appropriate government official. For your first trip to obtain your referral and meet a child, only one parent is required to travel, though most families have both parents travel (you will need a power of attorney from the spouse remaining in the US if only one parent goes).

Once in your selected region, you will meet with the appropriate government official and obtain the referral to meet a child. You will then travel to the orphanage to meet a child or children. You will be given medical and other information to review and will have a chance to interact with the child/children and establish a personal bond. This will give you time to consider your decision. You will not be forced to select a child.

When you have made the decision to accept the child, you will sign the Petition for Adoption. The next step is to submit your Petition for Adoption to the Regional Court along with the other appropriate documents.

Waiting Time

After accepting and bonding with your child, you may find it very difficult to endure the wait to complete the adoption. This is a stressful time. You must leave your new child behind you as you return to your home while the paperwork is processed in Russia. Use this time to redirect your thoughts to more productive things. It is good to know now that Russian adoption is a two-sided process. Up to this point, you have provided almost all of the necessary documents to the Russian Government to allow them detailed information explaining your side of the adoption. Your documents will give great detail about your ability and desire to adopt a child. Now the process shifts to the other side where it must be shown that the child has the legal status to be adopted. It will also be necessary for the Court to understand the child's health condition and social status, among other things, to conclude that the adoption is in the best interest of this particular child.

The Russian process begins with the Regional Operator of Databank of Children submitting a written request to the Federal Operator of Databank. The response will indicate that the information about the child to be adopted has been in the State Databank of Children not less than three months. The Regional Operator of Databank of Children has ten days to send this request, but in reality, most regions try to expedite this process so the time frame is usually less, two to three days on average. The Federal Operator of Databank also has ten days to send their response to the Regional Operator, but it can take longer for various reasons. During this interim time, the Inspector of the Body of Trusteeship and Guardianship will work to complete the necessary paperwork that is required by law to submit to the Court prior to the Court hearing.

The documents listed here are what must be prepared, reviewed and completed by the Department of Education authorities in every adoption case. You are not responsible for providing these documents:

1. Verification that the child's information has been in the State Databank of Children for the required time of not less than three months as stated by the letter from the Federal Operator of Databank.

2. A Report of the Bodies of Trusteeship and Guardianship about the propriety and compliance of the adoption with the interests of the child being adopted.

3. The birth certificate of the child being adopted.

4. A medical report on the state of health, and physical and mental development of the child being adopted.

5. The consent of the child (who is ten years of age or older) to be adopted, and also to possible changes in his (her) name, patronymic name, and surname and to recording the adoptive parents (parent) as his (her) parents (except for the cases, when such consent is not required under the law).

6. The consent of the parents of the child to his (her) adoption or the document confirming the Court decision if they are unknown or recognized by Court as missing; if they are recognized by Court as incapable or if their parental rights are removed by the Court, or the death certificate of the parents.

7.   The consent to adoption of the child's guardian (trustee), the foster parents or the head of the institution, in which a child who has been left without parental custody is being held.

Time frames for this process can vary due to each case having its own set of circumstances.

Finalizing Your Adoption

Russian Adoption must be finalized in a court hearing. Both parents must be present (the exception of course is with single parent adoptions). After the hearing, one parent may leave to return home. The court hearing can take a half-hour or could take two days in extreme cases. The Judge is then required to be alone to make his/her decision either by leaving the courtroom or asking others to leave, reconvening a little later to render the decision of the Court. (More comprehensive information in the section: Court Hearing).

It is important to note that Russian adoption laws protect the privacy of adoptive parents and adoptive children. Russia even legally terms this "Privacy of Adoption." The law protects these rights so strictly that if anyone violates the confidentiality of adoption against the adoptive parents wishes, it is considered a criminal offense. This is one of the reasons that adoption hearings are closed to anyone other than adoptive parents, government officials (Judge, Prosecutor, Orphanage Director, Body of Trusteeship and Guardianship) and your representative.

Child's Documents in the Regions

You will receive the Court decision (several copies) soon after the Court Hearing if the Judge decides to waive the 10 day waiting period, or after 10 days if not. When you have the Court decision in hand you will then need to obtain a Certificate of Adoption, a new Birth Certificate (with child's new name and your names listed as the parents) and Child's Passport.

The first step to obtain the child's documents is to go to the Body of Civil State Registration, commonly known as ZAGS (Zapis Actov Grazhdanskogo Sostoyaniya). This organization is similar to the US Office (Bureau) of Vital Statistics. From them you will obtain a Certificate of Adoption and a new Birth Certificate. As soon as you obtain these documents you will then go to the OVIR office (this is similar to a US Passport Office) and obtain your child's Passport. You will have to pay a government fee for the Passport and a government fee for a Passport "blank" (all together about $10 US).

The standard Passport process takes thirty days, but the law gives you rights to expedite this process. In most regions you will have to pay a separate regional fee for expediting this of $5-$15 (this can vary from region to region). Time frames can also differ, even with the expedited process. In some regions you can obtain your child's passport the same day you apply. Other regions may require up to three days.

Once you receive the new passport you are free to leave for Moscow. However, there are some other documents that you must obtain and have translated into English before going to the US Embassy in Moscow. Please note, if you are adopting in Sakhalin, Kamchatka, Magadan, Amur and Irkutsk regions or Khabarovsk and Primosrk Territories, you can process through the US Consulate in Vladivostok.

Before you leave the region, in addition to the Certificate of Adoption, the new Birth Certificate and the Passport, you will need additional documents for the US Embassy to apply for your child's Immigrant Visa. These additional documents you will obtain from the Orphanage, Body of Trusteeship and Guardianship or the Court. Please do check each of the additional documents very carefully to be sure they are certified originals and has a statement that it is a true and correct copy and has a signature and a blue "seal."

Since you will need to have all of these documents translated into English from Russian, it is recommended that you take care of this in the region before you leave. It will be much less expensive than having it done in Moscow.

This is the list of documents you will have to provide for the US Embassy. These must be originals (or certified copies) and they must be translated into English.

1. A certified copy of the child's original birth certificate, i.e. the one with the birth parents listed.

2. Information on the resolution of the birth parents' rights: death certificates, certificates certifying that the listed parents were not legally registered, letters of relinquishment, Court decrees removing parental rights, etc. If the child was a foundling and /or the orphanage has been unable to locate the child's parents, there should be certified copies of any official documents such as records of the orphanage's attempts to track the parents.

3. A letter from the orphanage or hospital that the child has resided in. This letter should include the dates of the child's stay in the institution, any information as to whether the child was visited and a statement of no objection to the adoption by the orphanage authorities.

4. A document confirming the availability of the information about the child being adopted in the State Databank of Children Without Parental Custody, confirming the impossibility of placing the child for care in the family of the citizens of the Russian Federation, continuously residing within the Russian Federation (commonly called the "release" letter from the Federal Operator of Databank).

5. The Adoption Court decision.

6. The Adoption Certificate.

7. The amended Birth Certificate, i.e. the one that indicates your names as parents.

Each official Russian document must be presented in the following way: The original document or a copy certified by the custodian of the document first followed by an English translation, one photocopy of the original and a second translation. Translations from languages other than Russian must be notarized.

Child's Immigrant Visa

Even after the adoption is complete, though you are listed as the parents of the child, this child is still considered a Russian Citizen. In order to enter the United States, the child will need a US Visa.

Before you can apply for the child's Visa to go to the United States, you must arrange a medical examination for the child. The US Embassy maintains a current list of doctors and sources for medicines should either you or your child experience health problems while in Russia.

You will need to supply a photograph of the child at the medical exam. This may be any color or black and white photo of your child. You may wish to get an extra photograph when you have your child's passport photos taken.

You may go to any of the following four authorized clinics in Moscow to complete the medical examination for your child's immigrant visa interview. You may want to check with the US Embassy for any new options:

FILATOV CLINIC
Sadovaya-Kudrinskaya Street, 15
103001 Moscow, Russia
(7-095) 423-7780 telephone, (7-095) 423-7780 fax
Appointment hours: 24 hour a day service available by appointment, Monday-Sunday
Medical examination for adopted orphans and other applicants under 15 years: $95
Medical examination for applicants 15 years and older: $95
e-mail: drsevps@online.ru (for adoption questions only)

AO "MEDITSINA"
Metro Mayakovskaya
2nd Tverskoy-Yamskoy Pereulok, Blvd. 10, rm. 420
125047 Moscow, Russia
(7-095) 250-9190, 250-9900, 250-9903, telephone
(7-095)250-9180 fax
Appointment hours: Monday-Friday: 8:00-20:00
Saturday-Sunday: 9:00-15:00
Medical examination for adopted orphans and other applicants under 15 years: $75
Medical examination for applicants 15 years and older: $100

INTERNATIONAL ORGANIZATION FOR MIGRATION (IOM)
No. 12 2nd Zvenigorodskaya, 1st entrance
Moscow
Metro: Ulitsa 1905 Goda
(7-095) 797-8723
Appointment hours: Monday-Thursday: 9:00-18:00
Friday: 9:00-16:30
Medical examination for adopted orphans and other applicants: $70
Medical examination for applicants 15 years and older: $70

AMERICAN MEDICAL CENTER
#1, Grokholsky per., Moscow
metro "Prospect Mira"
tel. 9337700
Those residing in Vladivostok ?onsular district (Amor, Sakhalin, Kamchatka, Magadan and Irkutsk regions, Khabarovsk and Primorsk territories) may obtain medical reports at:

CHILDREN'S HOSPITAL # 1 VLADIVOSTOK
#35, Okeansky prospect,Vladivostok 690090
Dr. Luchaninova V.N.
tel. 25-9335 or 25-2426

After completing the medical examination, you will receive a sealed envelope for the US Embassy containing the child's medical information. Do not open this. You are now ready to proceed to the US Embassy to submit all of the documents and process out.

The US Embassy states that they will not begin processing until your documents are complete. To ensure that they are able to help you process the visa for your adopted child as quickly as possible, please be sure that your documents are well organized and that forms OF-230 and I-600 are completed prior to your arrival at the Embassy. You may obtain information about and download these forms by visiting the INS website at: *http://www.ins.usdoj.gov.*

You will have to provide two sets of documents for each child being adopted. The first set is the original or certified copies with attached translations and the second is simply a copy of the first set.

The copies and translations will become part of the child's Immigrant Visa. All originals that are presented at the Embassy will be returned to you immediately following the interview with the consular officer.

It is advised that you check with the US Embassy prior to your arrival to be sure of any changes or additions to the process. The website (*www.usembassy.state.gov/moscow*) gives you all of the details of the processing times and their up-to-date information for the US Embassy. From time to time this information can change so you may wish to check regularly.

The U.S. Embassy in Moscow is located at:

#19/23, Novinsky Boulevard
Moscow, Russia 123242
728-5000 switchboard
728-5567, 728-5058, orphan visas
728-5247 fax

When processing out of Vladivostok, even though the medical exam and consular interview is handled locally, it will be required that you, your spouse or anyone that you provide with a Power of Attorney travel to Moscow to get the child's Visa.

The US Consulate in Vladivostok is located at:

#32 Pushkinskaya Street
Vladivostok, Russia 69001
Phone #7-(4232)-30-00-70; 7-(4232)-26-84-58
Fax (main): 7-(4232)-30-00-91
International Tel/Fax: 7-(509)-851-1011

Processing Out, Returning and Citizenship

The Child Citizenship Act (CCA), which became effective on February 27, 2001, represents a significant and important change in the nationality laws of the United States. Under the new law, most foreign-born children adopted by U.S. citizens will automatically acquire U.S. citizenship on the date they immigrate to the United States. In the past, adoptive parents had to apply for naturalization for their foreign-born children, who did not acquire citizenship until the Immigration and Naturalization Service (INS) approved the application. On occasion, delays in the old application process left adopted children subject to deportation from the United States. The change made by the CCA to automatic acquisition of citizenship by operation of law permanently protects the adopted children of U.S. citizens from deportation.

This process is being re-engineered and streamlined for the process of actually receiving a Certificate of Citizenship. In the interim, parents who would like to wait for the re-engineered process before filing for a Certificate of Citizenship but wish to have documentation of their child's status as a citizen may file for a U.S. Passport.

Here are some frequently asked questions taken from the official INS website:

<u>What type of child qualifies for automatic citizenship under the CCA?</u>

Under the CCA, a child will automatically acquire U.S. citizenship on the date that all of the following requirements are satisfied:

- ❑ At least one adoptive parent is a U.S. citizen,

- ❑ The child is under 18 years of age,

- ❑ There is a full and final adoption of the child, and

- ❑ The child is admitted to the United States as an immigrant

Is automatic citizenship provided for adopted children living outside the United States?

No. In order for a foreign-born child living outside the United States to acquire citizenship, the U.S. citizen parent must still apply for naturalization on behalf of the child. The naturalization process for such a child cannot take place overseas. The child will need to be in the United States temporarily to complete naturalization processing and take the oath of allegiance.

To be eligible, a child must meet the following requirements:

- ❑ The child has at least one U.S. citizen parent (by birth or naturalization);

- ❑ The U.S. citizen parent has been physically present in the United States for at least five years, at least two of which were after the age of 14; or the U.S. citizen parent has a citizen parent who has been physically present in the United States for at least five years, at least two of which were after the age of 14;

- ❑ The child is under 18 years of age;

- ❑ The child is residing outside the United States in the legal and physical custody of the U.S. citizen parent;

❑ The child is temporarily present in the United States–having entered the United States lawfully and maintaining lawful status in the United States; and

❑ The child must meet the requirements applicable to adopted children under immigration law.

If the naturalization application is approved, the child must take the same oath of allegiance administered to adult naturalization applicants. If the child is too young to understand the oath, INS may waive the oath requirement.

<u>Is automatic citizenship provided for those who are 18 years of age or older?</u>

No. Individuals who are 18 years of age or older on February 27, 2001, do not qualify for citizenship under the CCA, even if they meet all other criteria. If they wish to become U.S. citizens, they must apply for naturalization and meet eligibility requirements that currently exist for adult lawful permanent residents.

Registration of Your Child with the Russian Consulate

All children adopted from Russia must be registered with the Consulate Office of the Russian Federation. The appropriate office for registration will depend on your place of residence.

To register the adopted child the adoptive parents shall produce the following documents at a consular office:

1) the petition for the adopted child's registration and two photographs of the child;

2) the certificate of adoption;

3) the identification documents of the adoptive parents and the child (Passports).

The information about the child shall be entered into the registration card, the form which is approved by the Ministry of Foreign Affairs of the Russian Federation.

The consular office will put the registration stamp in the passport of the adopted child.

The registration of the adopted child may be executed before the child's exit out of the Russian Federation through the Department of Consular Service of the Ministry of Foreign Affairs of the Russian Federation (*address below).

If you choose this option, the aforementioned department shall transmit the petition of the adoptive parents for the adopted child's registration, the child's registration card and the photographs to the consular office corresponding to the place of residence of the adoptive parents and shall put the registration stamp in the passport of the child.

If your place of residence changes, you are required to inform the consular office at which the adopted child is registered and to register the child at the consular office corresponding to the new place of residence.

Website: *www.russianembassy.org*

Address: 32/34 Smolenskaya-Sennaya Pl.
Moscow 121200

Website: *www.mid.ru*

Post-Placements

One of the first documents you provided to the Russian authorities was a written obligation to allow your homestudy agency and its representatives to monitor the upbringing and living conditions of your adopted child. Also, your homestudy agency provided a written obligation to the Russian authorities to monitor the upbringing and living conditions of each of child adopted by you. It is a very important for this process and your obligation to be followed to the letter.

From time to time, Russian government authorities, such as the Regional Prosecution Department, monitor Post Placements and other activities required by Russian Law. Finding violations places a great amount of pressure on the authorities that assist in the adoption process (the same people who help you complete your adoption). When violations occur, it creates skepticism and problems, and reprimands or punishments for those workers responsible for these reports may occur because of their inability to provide these reports on the children adopted in their region. Please take this responsibility seriously and provide the post-placement reports in a timely fashion.

Article 16 of the Regulation of the Russian Government # 268 dated March 28, 2000 outlines the timeframes for Post Placement reports to be submitted to the proper authorities:

The first report must be provided six months after the adoption court decision has been legally in force, then six months after the first report and then annually for the next two years. If the appropriate Body of Executive Power of the Russian Federation should conclude that there is the necessity for continuation of supervision over the conditions of life and education of the child up to his/her legal age, then continued supervision and providing reports according to the decision of the appropriate Body of Executive Power of the Russian Federation would be necessary.

Post-placement reports must be notarized and Apostilled and translated into Russian. Translations of reports will be certified by a Notary in the Consulate of the Russian Federation in the USA or by a Notary in the territory of the Russian Federation.

Chapter Five

Dossier

A dossier is the packet of documents that is presented to the Russian government in support of your petition to adopt. Two sets of documents are required in most regions. One set goes to the Regional or Federal Operator of the Databank of Children Without Parental Custody. The second set of documents is filed with the Regional Court.

To be legal in Russia, all submitted original documents and all document copies must be notarized and Apostilled

Lists of Documents
(By Russian Legislation)

Here are two lists of the documents required by the appropriate government agencies in Russia. A detailed explanation of each follows:

FEDERAL/REGIONAL OPERATOR OF DATABASE

- Application for Federal/Regional Operator of Databank of Children Without Parental Custody

- The Questionnaire form (separate form for each adoptive parent)

- Parental Post Placement Commitment

- Parental Registration Commitment

- Copies of Passports (husband & wife)

- Homestudy with the family photo materials attached

- Agency's Post Placement Commitment

- Agency's Registration Commitment

- The Certified Copy of the License of the Homestudy Agency

THE REGIONAL COURT

- Court Application for Adoption

- Certified Copies of Passports (Husband & Wife)

- The Certified Copy of the Marriage Certificate (Birth Certificate – if single)

- Homestudy

- The Certified Copy of the License of the Homestudy Agency

- Agency's Post Placement Commitment

- Agency's Registration Commitment

- ❏ Employment Letter (Husband & Wife)

- ❏ Physician's Report (Husband & Wife)

- ❏ Police Clearance (Husband & Wife)

- ❏ Proof of Home Ownership or the Document Confirming the Right to Use the Living Quarters

- ❏ INS Approval

- ❏ Parental Post Placement Commitment

- ❏ Parental Registration Commitment

The adoption Judge has the right to require any additional documents.

Explanation of Documents

- ❏ **Application for Federal/Regional Operator of Database:** This petition contains your request to adopt the child and your request for the Federal/Regional Operator of Database to provide you with the information available in the State Databank about the child/ren meeting your criteria.

- ❏ **The Questionnaire Form**. This is a standard form, created by the Ministry of Education of the Russian Federation. When filled out it will contain your information to be put it into the database for registration as prospective adoptive parents. This form also specifies the number of children, ages and health status of children acceptable to you for consideration.

❑ **Homestudy:** This is a report from a licensed agency outlining the prospective adopters autobiographies and acknowledging that the prospective adopters have been assessed and found capable of parenting. Your social worker will interview you (typically there will be multiple interviews depending on your state's laws) and write an 8-15-page document, stating who you are, what you do, why s/he thinks you will make good parents. Your social worker will get this notarized for you. Your homestudy should be signed by your social worker and the director of the agency. This process can take from 3-8 weeks. Homestudy agencies must be approved for international adoptions. There are no Russian "accreditation" requirements for homestudy agencies.

❑ **Agency's Post Adoption Commitment:** A statement from the agency accepting responsibility for post-placement reports. This report will come from the same agency through which the social worker operates.

❑ **Agency's Registration Commitment:** This is a statement written by the homestudy agency which commits to reminding, instructing and overseeing the adoptive parents' responsibility to register their adopted child/ren with the Consulate Office of the Russian Federation within three months of returning home.

❑ **Parental Post Placement Commitment:** This is a statement similar to the agency's post-adoption commitment, stating that the parents will allow the agency to monitor the upbringing and living conditions of their adopted child/ren and provide to the appropriate Russian departments written post-placement reports.

❑ **Parental Registration Commitment:** This is a letter similar to the agency's registration commitment, verifying that the adoptive parents will fulfill their responsibility to register the child/ren with the Consulate Office of the Russian Federation. Registration is the responsibility of the parents. The agency only commits to remind and instruct the parents to complete this obligation.

❑ **Copy of Marriage Certificate:** This certificate must be certified and apostilled within the state of origin. Most states require that you obtain the certificate through a State government office rather than through local offices in order for it to be apostilled. In most States it is through the Secretary of State that you get your documents apostilled.

For a complete listing of Vital Records offices for each State.
http://catalog.com/fwcfc/vitalrec.html#top

❑ **Passport Photocopies (for each prospective adoptive parent):** Make sure that the passports will not expire until your adoption is complete (if your passport is within 6 months of expiring you are strongly advised to apply for a new passport). Make copies of the first two pages. You can make copies of both passports on a single page.

❑ **Medical Examination:** This document is completed by your physician and is good for three months. If it expires, it must be updated before the adoption court date.

❑ **Employment Verification Letter for Each Spouse Employed:** This is a letter on your company's letterhead stating your position, the number of years employed, your salary, and that you are an employee in good standing. If you are self-employed your accountant will need to write this up on his/her stationary. If you do not have an accountant, find one who will do it based on your W-2 form, or income tax return.

❏ **Proof of Home Ownership or the Document Confirming the Right to Use the Living Quarters.** If you own your home you will be required to submit a letter from the Bank or Mortgage Company verifying home ownership. You may also have to provide proof of home ownership from the county assessor. Make sure the letter lists the number of rooms and square footage of the interior and exterior property. Some regions require you to provide the copy of your deed. If you are renting or leasing your home, you will need to provide a statement from the property owner stating that you have legal rights to your living quarters.

❏ **Police Clearance:** This is a letter of good conduct on police letterhead.

❏ **Copy of INS Approval (I-171H):** Notice of Favorable Determination sent by INS approving your I-600A.

Notarization of Documents

Notarization is an important part of the process when preparing your dossier. You will have to gather documents from sources where a notary may not be available on site. You should call ahead of time and find out if you need to bring a notary public with you to verify the signatures. For example, you will likely have to bring a notary with you when requesting the police clearance letter from your local police or sheriff's office. Most police departments do not have notaries on staff. In these cases, you will need to be prepared and it is best to find a notary that is willing and able to accompany you for the notarization.

Below are samples of how to make statements for notarization.

IMPORTANT: (**Please check with your state to be sure you are following the required guidelines**)

FOR A CERTIFIED COPY:

STATE OF:_____

COUNTY OF:_____

On this _____ day of _____ 20 ___, I attest that the preceding or attached document is a true, exact, complete, and unaltered photocopy made by me of *(description of document)* presented to me by the document's custodian, *(name of custodian),* and, to the best of my knowledge, that the photocopied document is neither a public record nor a publicly recordable document, certified copies of which are available from an official source other than a notary public.

_____

Notary Public
Commission expires _____
(Notary Seal)

FOR AN ACKNOWLEDGEMENT IN AN INDIVIDUAL CAPACITY:

STATE OF:_____

COUNTY OF: _____

The foregoing instrument was acknowledged before me this _____ day of _____ 20 ___, by *(name of person acknowledging)*.

_____
Notary Public
Commission expires _____
(Notary Seal)

FOR OATH OR AFFIRMATION:

STATE OF:_____

COUNTY OF: _____

Sworn to (or affirmed) and subscribed before me this _____ day of _____ 20 ___, by *(name of person making statement)*.

_____
Notary Public
Commission expires _____
(Notary Seal)

Apostille

The Apostille is a document that certifies the veracity of the Notary Public signature. The Apostille is attached as a cover sheet to any document that is to be used in any country that has signed the 1961 Hague Convention Abolishing the Requirement of Legalization for Foreign Public Documents (Convention de La Haye du 5 Octobre 1961.). With an Apostille, the document is entitled to recognition in the country of intended use.

Documents issued in one country that need to be used in another country must be "authenticated" or "legalized" before they can be recognized as valid in the foreign country. This is a process in which various seals are placed on the document. Such documents range from powers of attorney, affidavits, birth, death and marriages records, incorporation papers, deeds, patent applications, home studies and other legal papers. The number and type of authentication certificates you will need to obtain depend on the nature of the document and whether or not the foreign country is a party to the multilateral treaty on "legalization" of documents.

(A) If your document is intended for use in a country which is a party to a treaty called the Hague Convention Abolishing the Requirement of Legalization for Foreign Public Documents ("Hague Legalization Convention", countries listed below), obtaining a special "Apostille" certificate is generally all that is required.

(B) If the country where the document will be used is not a party to the Convention, you will have to begin the cumbersome, time-consuming process of obtaining a series of certifications known as the "chain authentication method". This is literally a paper chase in which authorities will have to attest to the validity of a succession of seals beginning with your document and ending with the seal of the foreign embassy or consulate in the United States.

Since October 15, 1981, the United States has been part of the 1961 Hague Convention Abolishing the Requirement of Legalization for Foreign Public Documents. The Convention provides for the simplified certification of public (including notarized) documents to be used in countries that have joined the convention (see list of countries). Documents destined for use in participating countries and their territories should be certified by one of the officials in the jurisdiction in which the document has been executed. Said official must have been designated as competent to issue certifications by "Apostille" (usually in the office of the State Secretary of State of his/her counterpart) as provided for by the 1961 Hague Convention. The text of the Convention may be found in T.I.A.S. 10072; 33 U.S. Treaty Series (UST) 883; 527 U.N. Treaty Series (UNTS) 189, and Martindale-Hubble International Law Digest.

With this certification by the Hague Convention Apostille, the document is entitled to recognition in the country of intended use, and no certification by the Authentications Office or legalization by the embassy or consulate of the foreign country where the document is to be used is required. The Authentications Office only certifies documents from other Federal agencies and officials from foreign governments with the Apostille.

Purpose: The convention abolishes the requirement of diplomatic and consular legalization for public documents originating in one Convention country and intended for use in another. Documents issued in a Convention country that have been certified by a Convention Apostille are entitled to recognition in any other Convention country without any further authentication. Such recognition is an obligation on the part of the United States to the other countries party to the Convention and the Federal Courts and State authorities have been alerted to this obligation. Consular officers in Convention countries are prohibited from placing a certification over the Convention Apostille.

What Are Public Documents? For Convention purposes, public documents include:

(a) documents emanating from an authority or an official connected with the courts or tribunals of the State, including those emanating from a public prosecutor, a clerk of Court or a process server;

(b) administrative documents;

(c) notarial acts; and

(d) official certificates which are placed on documents signed by persons in their private capacity, such as official certificates recording the registration of a document or the fact that it was in existence on a certain date and official and notarial authentication of signatures.

HAGUE CONVENTION MEMBER COUNTRIES IN FORCE: ANDORRA, ANGOLA, ANGUILLA, ANTIGUA AND BARBUDA, ARGENTINA, ARMENIA, ARUBA, AUSTRALIA, AUSTRIA, BAHAMAS, BARBADOS, BELARUS, BELGIUM, BELIZE, BERMUDA, BOSNIA-HERZEGOVINA, BOTSWANA, BRITISH ANTARCTIC TERRITORY, BRITISH VIRGIN ISLANDS, BRUNEI, BUL-

GARIA, CAYMAN ISLANDS, COMOROS ISLANDS (formerly Moroni), CROATIA, CYPRUS, DJIBOUTI (formerly Affars and Issas), DOMINICA, EL SALVADOR, FALKLAND ISLANDS, FIJI, FINLAND, FRANCE, FRENCH GUIANA, FRENCH POLYNESIA, GUADELOUPE, GERMANY, GIBRALTAR, GREECE, GRENADA, GUERNSEY (Bailiwick of), HONG KONG, HUNGARY, ISLE OF MAN, ISRAEL, ITALY, JAPAN, JERSEY (Bailiwick of), KIRIBATI (formerly Gilbert Islands), LATVIA, LESOTHO, LIECHTENSTEIN, LUXEMBOURG, MACAO, MACEDONIA, MALAWI, MALTA, MARSHALL ISLANDS, MARTINIQUE, MAURITIUS, MEXICO, MONTSERRAT, MOZAMBIQUE, NETHERLANDS, NETHERLANDS ANTILLES (Curacao, Bonaire, St. Martin, St. Eustatius and Saba), NEW CALEDONIA, NORWAY, PANAMA, PORTUGAL, REUNION, RUSSIAN FEDERATION, ST. CHRISTOPHER (Kitts) AND NEVIS, ST. GEORGIA AND SOUTH SANDWICH ISLANDS, ST. HELENA, ST. LUCIA, ST. PIERRE AND MIQUELON, ST. VINCENT AND THE GRENADINES, SAN MARINO, SEYCHELLES, SLOVENIA, SOLOMON ISLANDS (formerly British Solomon Islands), SOUTH AFRICA, SPAIN, SURINAME, SWAZILAND, SWITZERLAND, TONGA, TURKEY, TURKS AND CAICOS, TUVALU (formerly Ellice Islands), UNITED KINGDOM, UNITED STATES, VANUATU (formerly New Hebrides), WALLIS AND FUTUNA.

State Authentication Authorities: (This list of State authorities was valid effective 4/1/97. See also 28 U.S.C.A., Fed. R. Civ. P. 44, pp. 328-31 (1992 & West Supp. 1993). It is valid for chain authentication and Hague Legalization Convention "Apostille" procedures.

Dossier

1. Alabama
Office of the Secretary of State
State Capitol Bainbridge St.
Montgomery, AL 36130
334-242-7205
Fee: $5.00
Designated Authority: Secretary of State

2. Alaska
Lieutenant Governor
P.O. Box 110015
Juneau, AK 99811
907-465-3509
Fee: $2.00
Designated Authority: Lieutenant Governor; Attorney General;
Clerk of the Supreme Court

3. Arizona
Office of the Secretary of State
Public Services Department
7th Floor 1700 W. Washington
Phoenix, AZ 85007
602 542-4086
Fee: $3.00
Designated Authority: Secretary of State; Assistant Secretary of State.

4. Arkansas
Office of Secretary of State
Notary Division State Capitol
Little Rock, AR 72201-1094
501-682-3409
Fee: $10.00
Designated Authority: Secretary of State; Chief Deputy Secretary of
State.

5. *California*
Office of the Secretary of State
P.O. Box 942877
Sacramento, CA 94277-0001
916-653-3595
Fee: $20.00
Designated Authority: Secretary of State; any Assistant Secretary of State; any Deputy Secretary of State.

6. *Colorado*
Office of Secretary of State
1560 Broadway Suite 200
Denver, CO 80202
303-894-2680
Fee: By Mail: $2.00 While You Wait: $17.00
Designated Authority: Secretary of State; Deputy Secretary of State.

7. *Connecticut*
Office of the Secretary of State
Authentications
30 Trinity St.
Hartford, CT 06106
203-566-5273
Fee: $20.00
Designated Authority: Secretary of State; Deputy Secretary of State.

8. *Delaware*
Office of Secretary of State Notary Division
P.O. Box 898
Dover, DE 19903
302-739-3077 or 302-739-3756
Fee: $10.00
Designated Authority: Secretary of State; Acting Secretary of State.

9. District of Columbia
Office of the Secretary, D.C.
Notary Commissions & Authentications Section
441 4th St. N.W. (One Judiciary Square)
Washington, D.C.
202-727-3117
Fee: $10.00
Designated Authority: Executive Secretary; Assistant Executive Secretary; Mayor's Special Assistant and Assistant to the Executive Secretary; Secretary of the District of Columbia.

10. Florida
Department of State Bureau of Notaries Public
The Capitol Building, Suite 1801
Tallahassee, FL 32399-0250
904-413-9732
Fee: $10.00
Designated Authority: Secretary of State

11. Georgia
Secretary of State Notary Division
2 Martin Luther King Drive
West Tower, Suite 820
Atlanta, GA 30334
404-656-2899
Fee: $3.00
Designated Authority: Secretary of State; Notary Public Division Director.

12. Hawaii
Office of the Lieutenant Governor
Box 3226, Honolulu, HI 96802
808-586-0255
Fee: $1.00
Designated Authority: Lieutenant Governor of the State of Hawaii.

13. Idaho
Office of Secretary of State
Box 83720
Boise, ID 83720
208-334-2300
Fee: $10.00
Designated Authority: Secretary of State; Chief Deputy Secretary of State; Deputy Secretary of State; Notary Public Clerk.

14. Illinois
Office of the Secretary of State Index Department
111 E. Monroe St.
Springfield, IL 62756
217-782-0646
Fee: $2.00
Designated Authority: Secretary of State; Assistant Secretary of State; Deputy Secretary of State.

15. Indiana
Office of Secretary of State
Statehouse Suite 201
Indianapolis, IN 46204
317-232-6542
Fee: $0.50
Designated Authority: Secretary of State; Deputy Secretary of State

16. Iowa
Office of Secretary of State Hoover Office Building
Second Floor
Des Moines, IA 50319
515-281-5204
Fee: $5.00
Designated Authority: Secretary of State; Deputy Secretary of State

17. Kansas

Office of Secretary of State
State Capitol, Second Floor
Topeka, KS 66612
913-296-2744
Fee: $5.00
Designated Authority: Secretary of State; Assistant Secretary of State; any Deputy Assistant Secretary of State.

18. Kentucky

Office of Secretary of State
Capitol Building P.O. Box 718
Frankfort, KY 40602-0178
502-564-7330
Fee: $5.00
Designated Authority: Secretary of State; Assistant Secretary of State.

19. Louisiana

Office of Secretary of State
P.O. Box 94125
Baton Rouge, LA 70804-9125
504-342-4981
Fee: $5.00
Designated Authority: Secretary of State.

20. Maine

Office of Secretary of State Bureau of Corporations
Elections and Commissions
Statehouse Station 101
Augusta, ME 04333
207-287-3676
Fee: $10.00
Designated Authority: Secretary of State; Deputy Secretary of State.

21. Maryland
Office of Secretary of State
Statehouse Annapolis, MD 21401
410-974-5520
Fee: $5.00
Designated Authority: Secretary of State.

22. Massachusetts
Deputy Secretary of the Commonwealth for Public Records
Room 1719
Commissions 1 Ashburton Place
Boston, MA 02108
617-727-2795
Fee: $3.00

23. Michigan
Department of State
Office of the Great Seal
Lansing, MI 48918-1750
517-373-2531
Fee: $1.00
Designated Authority: Secretary of State; Deputy Secretary of State.

24. Minnesota
Secretary of State's Office
180 State Office Bldg.
St. Paul, MN 55155
612-297-9102.
Fee: $5.00
Designated Authority: Secretary of State; Deputy Secretary of State.

25. Mississippi
Office of Secretary of State
P.O. Box 136
Jackson, MS 39205-0136
601-359-1615
Fee: $5.00
Designated Authority: Secretary of State; any Assistant Secretary of State.

26. Missouri
Office of Secretary of State Commission Division
P.O. Box 784
Jefferson City, MO 65102
314-751-2336
Fee: $10.00
Designated Authority: Secretary of State; Deputy Secretary of State.

27. Montana
Office of Secretary of State
Room 225, Box 202801
State Capitol
Helena, MT 59602
406-444-5379
Fee: $2.00
Designated Authority: Secretary of State; Chief Deputy Secretary of State; Government Affairs Bureau Chief.

28. Nebraska
Office of Secretary of State Notary Division
Room 1303 Box 95104
State Capitol Lincoln, NE 68509
402-471-2558
Fee: $10.00
Designated Authority: Secretary of State; Deputy Secretary of State.

29. Nevada
Secretary of State
101 N. Carson Street, #3
Carson City, NV 89701-4786
702-687-5203
Fee: $20.00
Designated Authority: Secretary of State; Chief Deputy Secretary of State; Deputy Secretary of State.

30. New Hampshire
Office of Secretary of State
Statehouse Room 204
Concord, NH 03301
603-271-3242.
Fee: $5.00
Designated Authority: Secretary of State; Deputy Secretary of State

31. New Jersey Department of State
Division of Commission Recording Notary Section
CN 452
Trenton, NJ 08625
609-530-6421
Fee: Regular Service: $25.00 Expedited Service: $35.00
Designated Authority: Secretary of State; Assistant Secretary of State

32. New Mexico
Office of the Secretary of State
State Capitol Building
Room 421
Santa Fe, NM 87503
505-827-3600
Fee: $3.00
Designated Authority: Secretary of State.

33. New York
1. Upstate Counties
Miscellaneous Records
162 Washington Ave.
Albany, NY 12231
518-474-4770
Fee: $10.00
Designated Authority: Secretary of State; Executive Deputy Secretary of State; any Deputy Secretary of State; any Special Deputy Secretary of State.

2. Down State Counties
New York authorities in Albany advise that documents issued in the nine down State counties are authenticated under the Convention by the New York City office. The nine down State counties are New York, Kings, Queens, Bronx, Westchester, Nassau, Suffolk, Rockland and Richmond. The address of the New York Department of State, Certification Unit is 6th Floor, 270 Broadway, New York, New York 10007, tel: 212-417-5684.
Fee: $10.00

34. North Carolina
Office of Secretary of State Authentication Division
300 N. Salisbury Street
Raleigh, N.C. 27603-5909
919-733-4129
Fee: $6.25
Designated Authority: Secretary of State; Deputy Secretary of State

35. North Dakota
Office of Secretary of State
Capitol Building, Bismarck, ND 58505
701-328-2900
Fee: $10.00
Designated Authority: Secretary of State; Deputy Secretary of State.

36. Ohio
Office of the Secretary of State
30 East Broad St., 14th Fl.
Columbus, OH 43266-0418
614-466-2585
Fee: $5.00
Designated Authority: Secretary of State; Assistant Secretary of State.

37. Oklahoma
Office of Secretary of State
2300 N. Lincoln, Room 101
Oklahoma City, OK 73105
405-521-4211
Fee: $25.00 (cashiers check or money order)
Designated Authority: Secretary of State; Assistant Secretary of State; Budget Officer of the Secretary of State.

38. Oregon
Office of Secretary of State
255 Capitol St. Suite 151
Salem OR 97310
503-986-2200.
Fee: $10.00
Designated Authority: Secretary of State; Deputy Secretary of State; Acting Secretary of State; Assistant to the Secretary of State.

39. Pennsylvania
Department of State Bureau of Commissions
Elections and Legislation
North Office Building Room 304
Harrisburg, PA 17120
717-787-5280
Fee: $15.00
Designated Authority: Secretary of the Commonwealth; Executive Deputy Secretary of the Commonwealth.

40. Rhode Island
Office of Secretary of State Notary Division
100 N. Main St.
Providence, RI 02903
401-277-1487
Fee: $5.00
Designated Authority: Secretary of State; First Deputy Secretary of State; Deputy Secretary of State

41. South Carolina
Office of Secretary of State
P.O. Box 11350
Columbia, SC 29211
803-734-2119
Fee: $2.00
Designated Authority: Secretary of State

42. South Dakota
Office of Secretary of State
500 East Capitol
Pierre, SD 57501-5077
605-773-5004
Fee: $2.00
Designated Authority: Secretary of State; Deputy Secretary of State

43. Tennessee
Office of Secretary of State
James K. Polk Building
18th Floor
Nashville, TN 37243-0306
615-741-3699
Fee: $2.00
Designated Authority: Secretary of State.

44. Texas
Office of Secretary of State
P.O. Box 12079
Austin, TX 78711
512-463-5705
Fee: $10.00
Designated Authority: Secretary of State; Assistant Secretary of State

45. Utah
Office of the Lieutenant Governor
State Capitol Room 203
Salt Lake City, UT 84145-8414
801-538-1040
Fee: Certifying Notary's Seal: $10.00 Apostille: $5.00
Designated Authority: Lieutenant Governor; Deputy Lieutenant Governor; Administrative Assistant.

46. Vermont
Office of Secretary of State
109 State St.
Montpelier, VT 05609-1103
802-828-2308
Fee: $2.00
Designated Authority: Secretary of State; Deputy Secretary of State.

47. Virginia
Office of Secretary of Commonwealth
Authentications Division
P.O. Box 2454
Richmond, VA 23219
804-786-2441
Fee: $10.00
Designated Authority: Secretary of the Commonwealth; Chief Clerk, Office of the Secretary of Commonwealth.

48. Washington
Department of Licensing
Business and Professions Division Notary Section
P.O. Box 9027
Olympia, WA 98507-9027
360-586-4575
Fee: $15.00
Designated Authority: Secretary of State; Assistant Secretary of State; Director, Department of Licensing.

49. West Virginia
Office of Secretary of State
1900 Kanawha Blvd. East
Capitol Building No. 157-K
Charleston, WV 25305-0770
304-558-6000
Fee: $10.00
Designated Authority: Secretary of State; Under Secretary of State; any Deputy Secretary of State.

50. Wisconsin
Office of Secretary of State
P.O. Box 7848
Madison, WI 53707-7848
608-266-5503
Fee: $5.00
Designated Authority: Secretary of State; Assistant Secretary of State.

51. Wyoming
Office of Secretary of State
The Capitol
Cheyenne, WY 82002-0020
307-777-5342
Fee: $3.00
Designated Authority: Secretary of State; Deputy Secretary of State.

* Information of the US Department of State

Some States may have satellite offices also authorized to issue Apostilles under the authority of the respective State official.

Chapter Six

Court Hearing

The court hearing is the most important step in the adoption process. The court hearing itself may take anywhere from thirty minutes to two days.

Since all adoption proceedings are conducted in a closed hearing, the only people allowed in the courtroom will be the Judge, the Prosecutor, the Judicial Clerk, the adoptive parents, the Inspector of the Body of Trusteeship and Guardianship, the Director of the Orphanage, a translator and your adoption representative.

The Procedure of Court Hearing

The procedure of a judicial sitting is defined in chapter 15 of the Code of Civil Procedure of the Russian Federation.

When the Judge enters the courtroom all the people present in the courtroom stand up. Similarly, at the end of the hearing all those present in the courtroom stand while listening to the Judge pronounce the court decision. All who are in the courtroom shall follow the established order during the hearing and comply completely with the appropriate directions from the Judge (article 148 of the Code of Civil Procedure of the Russian Federation).

At the moment the Judge enters the courtroom and takes his/her chair the participants of the process start to exercise all the procedural rights and bear the responsibilities, which they are endued upon trial (article 150 of the Code of Civil Procedure of the Russian Federation).

The Judge explains to the interpreter his (her) duty to interpret the explanations, evidence, and statements of the persons who do not know the language of the court procedure and to explain to these persons the content of explanations, evidence, statements, and the read documents, as well as the directions of the Judge, and the definitions and Court decree. The Judge warns the interpreter about criminal liability (article 152 of the Code of Civil Procedure of Russian Federation).

The Judge outlines the composition of the Court, and informs the participants about those who presides as the Prosecutor, Interpreter, and Judicial Clerk and expounds to the persons involved in the case their right to appeal. The Judge asks whether or not you trust the Judge, Prosecutor and Judicial Clerk (article 154 of the Code of Civil Procedure of the Russian Federation).

The Judge explains to the participants their representatives their procedural rights and responsibilities, such as: to be instructed about the case, to give evidence, to proceed in the investigation, to ask other persons involved in the case, witnesses, and experts questions, to present a petition, to present the case orally and in writing, to produce arguments and considerations on all arising questions, to object to petitions, arguments and considerations of other persons proceeding in the case, to get to know the records of Court hearing and to comment on the records with specifying the cross-errors and imperfections within 3 days following the day of signing, the right of the participants proceeding in the case to appeal against the judgment to the Court of Appeal, and also the duty of the people proceeding in the case to exercise in good faith their procedural rights. The Judge ascertains from the persons proceeding in the case their consent or objection to sole legal investigation (article 155 of the Code of Civil Procedure of the Russian Federation).

Before the Court investigation of the case the Judge ascertains from the persons proceeding in the case if there are any additional documents to submit (article 156 of the Code of Civil Procedure of the Russian Federation).

The court proceeding begins with the report of the Judge. The Judge reads the Application of the petitioners, and then asks whether their opinion and wish to adopt the child/children has changed or not (article 164 of the Code of Civil Procedure of the Russian Federation).

After the report, the Court hears the explanations of the petitioners. The Judge may ask which petitioner wishes to give evidence first or may choose one of the petitioners to answer first. The Judge will ask your full name, date of birth, place of residence, place of employment and position. Then the Judge will ask you to furnish details about yourself, your family, your decision to adopt the child, etc. The Judge and then the Prosecutor and the Representative of the petitioners will ask questions. Some Judges start to ask questions at once thereby helping the petitioner to escape unnecessary narration. The Judge will request the inspector of the Bodies of Trusteeship and Guardianship to give an opinion about the propriety and compliance of the adoption with the interests of the child. The Inspector may be asked questions by the Judge, Prosecutor, Petitioners and the Representative of the Petitioner (article 166 of the Code of Civil Procedure of the Russian Federation).

The next stage of the Court procedure is the investigation of documentary evidence. The Judge will examine the documents available in the case papers. These are all the documents that the petitioners submitted to the Court (the dossier) and also the child's documents the copies of which they will have after the judicial sitting (article 175 of the Code of Civil Procedure of the Russian Federation).

After considering all evidence, the Judge asks the adopting parents and their representative if they wish to add anything else to the documents already submitted. If there is no such submission the Judge declares the Court's investigation of the case closed and the Court passes on hearing the judicial debate and the opinion of the public prosecutor. At this stage you may add to your previous explanations. Usually at this stage it is necessary to present the petition for the prompt execution of the Court decision and to validate the request. Some Judges prefer this petition to be presented at the beginning of the judicial procedure (article 184 of the Code of Civil Procedure of the Russian Federation).

The next stage of the Court hearing is the judicial debate, which includes the speeches of participants in the case and their representative. At this stage of the judicial preceding the participants of the case analyze the results of judicial investigation, state their view of legal relations, and express their judgment about the decree that should be rendered. Usually at this stage the professional Attorney of the adoptive parents (if represented) takes the floor and competently justifies his (her) position. The adoptive parents may confine themselves to a simple petition for the adoption decree (article 185 of the Code of Civil Procedure of the Russian Federation).

After hearing the judicial debate the Prosecutor in the case gives his/her opinion. The Prosecutor must analyze in detail the sources of evidence investigated during the judicial proceeding, show which of them are to be recognized as trustworthy and which are not and why, comment on the law regulating the given legal relations, and give finally his/her opinion of the way the case has to be resolved under this regulation (article 187 of the Code of Civil Procedure of the Russian Federation).

After hearing the opinion of the Prosecutor, the Judge leaves the courtroom and goes to a private room to deliberate over the decree. Under the law the decree is deliberated in a room into which access is prohibited for any person. This procedure is designed to eliminate outside influence on the Judge while deliberating over the decree (article 189 of the Code of Civil Procedure of the Russian Federation).

The next stage is the announcement of the court decision. After writing and signing the decree the Judge comes back to the courtroom and announces the court decision. All those in attendance in the courtroom listen to the content of the decree and must remain standing, except those whom the Court has made exception for because of their state of health. The Judge reads the entire content of the court decision, followed by the procedure and the terms to file an appeal (article 190 of the Code of Civil Procedure of the Russian Federation).

Always address the Judge as "your Honor." It is not appropriate to address the Judge as "Ma'am" or "Sir."

Court Questions

It is likely that you will face a number of questions from the Court. These questions can vary in number and in content. What follows is a list of many of the commonly asked questions. It is a good idea to become familiar with these in advance of your court date. The number of questions can range from a few to many depending on the Judge and officials of the court and your particular case.

- ❑ Why did you decide to adopt?
- ❑ Why did you not adopt from your own country?
- ❑ Why did you choose Russia?
- ❑ What is your annual income?
- ❑ Do you own your house? Are you still paying for it?
- ❑ What's your house like?
- ❑ Are you positive that you have funds to raise a child?
- ❑ Have you prepared a nursery?
- ❑ What is the attitude of your family towards the adoption?
- ❑ Were you raised in a big family? Talk about your parents and siblings (no details – just how far they are from your home).

- Do you have any experience taking care of young children?

- What is your child-care plan?

- Who will do the biggest part of the work in taking care of the child?

- Will you help your wife/husband after work?

- Do you recognize corporal punishment as a method of disciplining children?

- What methods do you believe are appropriate for disciplining children?

- Do you have insurance? Will it cover the child? When?

- Are you aware of the legal consequences of adoption and in case it's terminated of the consequences of termination?

- Are you familiar with the Russian law concerning adoptions?

- Do you know that the social worker will be visiting you regularly? Will you provide access to your house?

- Will you register the child in the Russian consulate in the US?

- Do you have a legal custodian in case something unexpected happens to you? Who is the person? Is s/he married? Does s/he have children?

- What is your education?

- Do you smoke, take drugs, are you addicted to alcohol?

- Do you have a police clearance?

- Are you a healthy person? Did you go through a medical exam and what is the result?

- Are you aware of the child's state of health?

- Do you see any obstacles that could stop you from fulfilling parental responsibilities?

- How many times did you see the child you are adopting?

- Did you bond?

- Is it your first marriage? Is it a stable marriage? (If it is not the first marriage talk briefly for how long you had been married before and what the reason was for the divorce).

- According to the laws of your state, in case you divorce, who will take of the child?

- Will you render financial help?

- After your adoption if your child will develop a health problem that is not indicated in the record, will you have any claims against the orphanage or the Russian government?

- Will the decree of the Russian Court be recognized in your state?

- Are you going to obtain citizenship for the child in your country? How will you do it?

10 Days

Article 211 of the Code of Civil Procedure of the Russian Federation empowers the Judge to enforce any Court decision immediately in cases where the ten day wait may lead to a significant loss for the petitioner or the where the adoption itself may appear impossible.

In each particular case the court shall decide the necessity of immediate execution or the denial of it in the declaration, and shall specify the extent to which it is subject to immediate execution in the substantive provisions.

At the same time the petition itself does not predetermine the obligation of the Court to execute the Court decision immediately. The person submitting the petition shall validate and prove that the delay of execution will lead to a loss for the petitioner or to the impossibility of execution due to special circumstances.

If the Court decides on immediate execution of the decision, it shall go into effect immediately irrespective of an appeal or protest and cannot be stopped by any official or person filing a protest or appeal. You have the right to receive the copy of the Court decree and to apply to competent authorities for issuing the Adoption Certificate, the new Birth Certificate and the Passport.

Clause 17 of the Regulation of the Supreme Court Plenum of the Russian Federation enacted on July 4, 1997, # 9 gives an example of the circumstance which may be considered as exceptional: *the necessity of emergency hospitalization of the adopted child for a course of treatment and/or operative inter-*

vention, and the delay threatens the life and health of the child. Other grounds are not specified anywhere in the legislation, therefore in each particular case the Judge shall conclude which circumstances may be considered as exceptional and which may not.

Since Judges have different moral certainty, some of them consider practically all causes as exceptional (the necessity for the child to adjust in the family, the interview at the Embassy, the necessity for the adoptive parents to come back to work, the children of the adoptive parents left in their country and so on). Other Judges feel that these are personal problems of the adoptive parents that were known beforehand, and they cannot be considered as exceptional circumstances, which are the causes to enforce the decree immediately.

Chapter Seven

Russian Law (Translated)

CONSTITUTION
OF THE RUSSIAN FEDERATION
(Excerpts)

December 12, 1993 (With the amendments of January 9, 1996,
February 10, 1996 and June 9, 2000)

CHAPTER I

FUNDAMENTALS OF THE
CONSTITUTIONAL FRAMEWORK

Article 2

An individual and his (her) rights and freedoms are of the greatest value. The recognition, observance and protection of the rights and freedoms of an individual and citizen shall be the responsibility of the State.

Commentary to article 2

The article states one of the fundamentals of the Constitutional framework of the Russian Federation. In the Constitution, the concept of "the greatest value" is referring to an individual and his (her) rights and freedoms. It is characteristic that no other legal institution included into the concept of the fundamentals of the Constitutional framework is specified with such terms.

The proclamation of protection of the rights and freedoms of an individual and citizen also means it is the responsibility of the State to establish special institutions protecting human rights and freedoms. They include Courts, Bodies of Protection of Public Law and Order, Prosecutors' offices, and also Institutions of the Human Rights Authorized Agents. Every chapter of the Constitution provides the duty of the State to detail the rights and freedoms of an individual and citizen and to protect them by the force of the law. Thus, article 2 of the Constitution guarantees individual freedom and democracy and vitality of the State and society.

Article 4

2. The Constitution of the Russian Federation and Federal Acts has supremacy within the whole territory of the Russian Federation.

Commentary to article 4

This clause secures one of the major fundamentals of a Federative Lawful State directly following from the principle that the sovereignty of the Russian Federation covers all its territory. The supremacy of the Federal Constitution and Federal Acts within the whole territory of the Russian Federation ensures unity, consistency and stability of the entire legal system of Russia. It presumes their precise and strict observance, execution and enforcement. It implies the requirement for all statutory legal acts enacted by the President of the Russian Federation, the Government of the Russian Federation, and Federal Executive Bodies as well as Laws and other statutory legal acts enacted by the subjects of the Russian Federation on the matters of the Joint Administration of the Federation and its subjects to correspond exactly with the Constitution and Federal Acts. The said acts shall not be contrary to the Constitution and Federal Acts. If such contradiction (non-conformity) is discovered, the Constitution or the appropriate Federal Law is applied. The acts contradicting to them are subject to protestation, suspension or reversal in due order. As it follows from the meaning of this article of the Constitution, this rule acts within the whole territory of the Russian Federation.

Article 15

1. The Constitution of the Russian Federation shall have superior legal force and direct effect and shall be applied within the whole territory of the Russian Federation. Laws and other legal acts adopted in the Russian Federation shall not contradict the Constitution of the Russian Federation.

2. Public authorities, local authorities, officials, citizens and their unions shall observe the Constitution and laws of the Russian Federation.

3. Laws are subject to official promulgation. The unpublished laws may not be applied. Any statutory legal acts involving the rights, freedoms and duties of an individual and citizen may not be applied if they have not been promulgated for general notification.

4. The generally recognized principles and provisions of International law and the International Treaties of the Russian Federation are the constituent of its legal system. If an International Treaty of the Russian Federation establishes other rules than provided by the Law, the rules of the International Treaty shall be applied.

Commentary to article 15

This article is especially important because it determines the position of the Constitution in the system of statutory legal acts of the country. The Constitution forms and secures the starting principles of legal regulation; it is the foundation of all legislation and represents the act having superior legal force.

The laws and by-laws contradicting the Constitution have no legal force. Besides, not only the acts of Federal Legislation but also the Acts of Public Authorities of the Subjects of the Federation shall comply with the Constitution. Covering the whole territory of the Russian Federation the Constitution embodies State integrity and the unity of the State power system. The Constitution has direct effect. At the same time the text of the Constitution contains the indicated necessity to adopt a number of Federal Constitutional Laws and Federal Acts, the force of which shall provide the extension of provisions secured by the Constitution in general.

The Constitution and Laws of the Russian Federation regulate major public relations. With their help the fundamentals of the constitutional framework, the basic rights and freedoms of citizens, the state structure, forms and kinds of property, the fundamentals of the criminal, civil, family and other branches of legislation and also other fundamental aspects of vital activity of the society and State are ensured. The duty to observe Federal Legislative Acts covers accordingly all public authorities, including the authorities of the subjects of the Federation, local authorities, and also all the officials without distinction. The law-enforcement policy of all State Bodies shall comply with the Constitution, and officials, irrespective of their rank and position, shall be responsible in case of violation of Constitutional Provisions and Laws.

The Legislative Acts of the Russian Federation shall be in the same way indispensable for citizens and their associations. The overall obligation of such Acts follows from their potential perception as a measure of equity applied equally to all citizens.

It is necessary to mention that the force of the Constitution and Laws of the Russian Federation covers not only the citizens of Russia, but also foreign and stateless persons being in its territory (except as provided by the legislation in force).

It is extremely important for a law to be promulgated for general notification, as publicity in legislation directly involves the rights and legitimate interests of citizens and other subjects of Law. The knowledge of the law cannot be the privilege of the selected persons.

The process of the increasing openness of the Russian society could only affect the promulgation of statutory acts. In this area considerable changes have taken place secured by the constitutional provisions, according to which the promulgation of laws and other statutory acts are closely connected with their implementation.

The unpublished laws cannot be applied within the Russian Federation. Moreover, any statutory acts involving rights, freedoms and duties of citizens (these are governmental regulations and a great number of departmental acts) cannot be applied, if they are not officially promulgated for general notification. This Constitutional Provision means, in point of fact, that laws and other acts specified in clause 3 of this article (rather their full and exact texts) shall be announced in newspapers or special publications of rule-making bodies or under their instruction by other bodies.

According to the Federal Law called "About the Order of Promulgation and Implementation of Federal Constitutional Laws, Federal Acts, and the Acts of the Chambers of the Federal Assembly", enacted by the State Duma on May 25, 1994, the official promulgation of a Federal Constitutional Law, Federal Act, or an act of a Chamber of the Federal Assembly is the first publication of its full text in a "Russian Newspaper" or in the "Collection of the Legislation of the Russian Federation". Federal Constitutional Laws, Federal Acts, and the Acts of the Chambers of the Federal Assembly can be announced in other publications, and also promulgated on television and radio, sent to State Bodies, officials, enterprises, establishments and organizations, transmitted by communication systems and distributed in a machine-readable format.

Federal Constitutional Laws and Federal Acts are subject to official promulgation within seven days after the date of their enactment. International Treaties of the Russian Federation regulate the relations of Russia with Foreign States and International Organizations. They are concluded under the Constitution and Federal Acts on behalf of the Russian Federation by the authorized Federal Bodies. After official recognition, ratification and approval International Treaties acquire in due order a binding force within Russia.

Such Treaties are defined in the Federal Act called "About the International Treaties of the Russian Federation" enacted by the State Duma of June 16, 1995 and put into effect on July 21, 1995. So, "an International Treaty of the Russian Federation" means an International Agreement concluded by Russia with a Foreign State (or States) or with an International Organization in writing and regulated under International Law.

The International Treaties of the Russian Federation are concluded on behalf of the Russian Federation (Interstate Treaties), on behalf of the Government of the Russian Federation (Intergovernmental Treaties), or on behalf of Federal Executive Bodies (Interdepartmental Treaties). The International Treaties are the essential elements of International Law, order, stability and the relations of Russia with foreign countries. The Russian Federation stands out for strict observance of treaty and customary rules and sustains its adherence to the basic principle of International Law, the principle of fair execution of International responsibility.

In case of contradiction of a law or other statutory act to the International Treaty in which the Russian Federation participates, or to the generally recognized principles of International Law the rules established by these principles or by the treaty shall be applied.

According to the Constitution, everyone has the right under the International Treaties of the Russian Federation to apply to Human Rights Interstate Bodies when all the means of legal protection available within the State have been exhausted.

CHAPTER II

RIGHTS AND FREEDOMS OF INDIVIDUALS AND CITIZENS

Article 17

1. In the Russian Federation, the rights and freedoms of an individual and citizen shall be recognized and guaranteed in conformity with the generally recognized principles and provisions of International Law and under the Constitution.

2. The fundamental rights and freedoms of an individual shall be inalienable and shall belong to everyone from birth.

3. The exercise of rights and freedoms of an individual and citizen may not violate the rights and freedoms of other persons.

Commentary to article 17

The meaning and importance of this article is that the non-conformity of the condition of a person in the Russian Federation during past decades with the International principles relating to human rights has been finally overcome. Part 1 of

*the article recognizes principles and provisions of International-
al Law. Therefore, the Universal Declaration of Human
Rights, the International Covenants on Human Rights and all
Conventions on Rights and Freedoms ratified by Russia shall
be observed within the Russian Federation. The recognition of
rights of an individual and citizen by the State means the
responsibility of the State to affirm these rights in its legislation, preferably in the Constitution.*

*The rights of individual and citizen in the Russian Federa-
tion are universal. None of the subjects of the Federation can
deny the responsibility to recognize and guarantee the rights of
individual and citizen in its territory.*

*Clause 2 of article 17 declares all rights and freedoms of an
individual as fundamental. Their equivalence thereby is
acknowledged. Two properties of the fundamental rights are
defined here. One of them is their inalienability: none of the
rights of an individual and citizen declared in the Constitution
can be taken away by the State or restricted in capacity without specifying the grounds of restriction. The rights and freedoms of an individual may be restricted by the State only
subject to strictly defined cases under the Constitution and the
Law.*

*Temporary restrictions of some rights and freedoms are pos-
sible in case of introducing a state of emergency.*

*The Inalienability of Rights and Freedoms also means that
a citizen cannot take obligation to not use his (her) rights.
Such obligations are legally void. In case of violation of the
rights and freedoms of an individual and citizen they shall be
re-established by the appropriate State Bodies or Lawful Acts
of a person whose rights have been violated.*

The fact of an individual's birth is sufficient for the beginning of human rights. The enjoyment of rights and freedoms does not mean the possibility of unrestricted outrage in the exercise of someone's rights or of human rights abuse. The principle of respect of another person's rights and freedoms is inextricably connected with the idea of enjoying the fundamental rights. Therefore clause 3 of this article prohibits the violation of rights and freedoms of other persons while exercising one's own rights.

Article 19

1. All people shall be equal before the Law and in the Court of Law.

2. The State shall guarantee the equality of rights and freedoms of an individual and citizen regardless of sex, race, nationality, language, origin, property or employment status, residence, attitude to religion, convictions, membership of public associations or any other circumstance. Any restrictions of the rights of citizens on social, racial, national, linguistic or religious grounds shall be prohibited.

Commentary to article 19

The history of human rights development has revealed their inextricable connection with the national legislation and judicial protection.

Clause 1 of this article determines equal rights as the equality of everyone before the Law and in the Court. The Law as the act, enacted as a Constitutional Law or an Act of Legislation is the objectively indispensable remedy of formulating rights and freedoms. Therefore, the institution of equality before the law as a common standard (on an equal scale) determining individual freedom is so very important. The equality of everyone in the Court is extremely essential, as the Court is the most efficient means of protection and reinstatement in rights and freedoms in case of lawsuit or violation of their rights.

It is necessary to mention that the provision of clause 1, about the equality of everyone before the law and in the Court, means that this principle covers the citizens of the Russian Federation, citizens of other states and stateless persons. Clause 2 of this article determines equal rights as the equality of an individual and citizen in possessing rights and freedoms. This clause formulates the responsibility of the State to guarantee this equality without reference to both the physical qualities of a person and his (her) public features.

Sex, race and nationality are indicated as physical qualities of a person. Public features of a person include language, origin, property and employment status, residence, attitude to religion, convictions, and membership of public associations.

Clause 2 of this article also means that the article considers different features of an individual. Human dignity thereby receives legal protection from discrimination according to article 2 of the Universal Declaration of Human Rights, article 2 of the International Covenants on Human Rights and article 14 of the European Convention on Protection of Human Rights and Fundamental Freedoms. The enumeration of individual features in which discrimination is prohibited is not comprehensive. Clause 2 of this article specifies the possibil-

ity of also considering "other circumstances", which can arise in real life.

The Constitutional Principle is protected by article 136 of the Criminal Code, according to which deliberate acts offending against equal rights of citizens on racial, national, or religious grounds shall be punished with deprivation of freedom or fine.

Article 24

1. It shall be prohibited to gather, store, use and disseminate information on the private life of any person without his (her) consent.

2. Public authorities and the bodies of local self-government and the officials shall provide to each citizen access to any documents and materials directly affecting his (her) rights and freedoms unless otherwise provided under the law.

Commentary to article 24

In Russia, the problem of individual rights protection, while dealing with the information about citizens (personal data), was not considered important until recently. The modification of conceptual approaches to most phenomena of society life and, first of all, to their humanitarian aspects, has also affected the protection of citizens' rights including the protection of a person from the unauthorized collection of personal data and from abuse, which is possible during the collection, storage and dissemination of personal data.

The Constitution states the consent of a person to the collection, storage, usage and dissemination of the information about his (her) private life is compulsory. The Constitution prohibits the collection, storage, usage and dissemination of the information about his (her) private life without the person's permission. Therefore, it is possible to draw a conclusion that within the Russian Federation this protection shall be granted to any person whether this person is or is not a citizen of the Russian Federation.

Clause 1 of article 24 sets a general rule, which acts within the limits of enjoying the rights and freedoms established in the Constitution. So, the consent of a person to collecting, storing, using and disseminating his (her) personal information is not required when judicial investigation, inquisition, or field investigative activities are carried out.

Clause 1 of article 24 assigns the duty and obligation to provide to every citizen access to any documents and materials directly affecting his (her) rights and freedoms to public authorities, the bodies of local self-government and the officials.

The right granted by the Constitution to get access to any documents and materials directly affecting individual rights and freedoms is connected with some restrictions: only persons whose rights and freedoms are concerned may get access to such documents and materials.

Therefore, the set of persons is limited to directly interested persons, and the set of documents and materials is limited to only those documents that affect the rights and freedoms of the persons applying for the information.

There is one more restriction: the interested party may use the right granted to him except as otherwise provided under the law. It is necessary to point out the following: the exception is taken under the law, but not under any subordinate legislation. Therefore, if the authority or any official denies access to documents and materials and justifies the denial by the departmental instruction, but not by the law, such denial shall be qualified as contradicting to the Constitution and, therefore, subject to appeal by the interested party.

Article 27

1. Everyone who is lawfully staying within the Russian Federation shall have the right to freedom of movement and to choose the place to stay and reside.

Commentary to article 27

Each person shall be free to choose the place of permanent residence and the place of temporary stay. This provision covers only persons lawfully residing within the Russian Federation. The persons who have crossed the State boundary of the Russian Federation unlawfully do not have these rights, since their free movement within the State territory can do significant harm to public interest. However, if a foreign citizen has arrived lawfully in the State territory having a visa of the Russian Federation with the designation of one city (for example, Moscow), this person shall have the legal right to move within the Russian Federation visiting different regions before the visa expires.

Article 33

Citizens of the Russian Federation shall have the right to apply personally and also to send individual and collective petitions to State Bodies and local self-governments.

Commentary to article 33

In spite of the fact, the article designates that the citizens of the Russian Federation and both foreign and stateless persons shall have the right to turn to State Bodies. This right is ensured by the Constitution. There is also the Decree of the Presidium of the Supreme Soviet of the USSR of April 12, 1968, # 2534-VII «About the procedure of considering proposals, applications and petitions of citizens». Despite the fact that the Government of the Soviet Union enacted this Decree, it remains in force. It states that all State and Public Bodies shall accept and consider petitions of citizens within one month.

The Constitution provides the right to all citizens to apply personally and to send written petitions by mail.

Article 45

1. State protection of the rights and freedoms of an individual and citizen in the Russian Federation shall be guaranteed.

2. Everyone shall have the right to defend his or her rights and freedoms by any means not prohibited by the law.

Commentary to article 45

All State authorities (the President of the Russian Federation, the Government, the State Duma, etc.) shall respect and protect human rights and freedoms. According to article 2 of the Federal Law "About the Fundamentals of the Governmental Service" the Administrative Bodies shall follow in their activities the principle of keeping and respecting the rights of an individual and citizen.

All law-enforcement agencies such as Prosecutors' Offices, Militia, etc. are established and operate for this purpose.

Judicial protection is one of the major ways of ensuring the observance of human rights and freedoms.

Clause 2 of this article recognizes the right of every citizen to defend his or her rights and freedoms by any means not prohibited by the law. Everyone has the right to appeal for the protection of their rights and freedoms and to take legal action, to apply to public agencies, and to use mass media.

Article 46

1. Everyone shall be guaranteed protection of his or her rights and freedoms in the Court.

2. The decisions and actions (or inactions) of State bodies, local self-governments, public associations and any officials may be appealed in the Court.

3. In conformity with the International Treaties of the Russian Federation everyone shall have the right to apply to interstate organizations concerned with the protection of human rights and freedoms when all the means of legal protection available within the State have been exhausted.

Commentary to article 46

The article supports important democratic principles ensuring judicial protection of the rights and freedoms to each individual. It is formulated according to the International Treaties, including article 6 of the European Convention on Protection of Human Rights and Fundamental Freedoms.

Depending on the violated right, the protection may be realized with the Criminal, Administrative, Civil or Constitutional Court procedure. The current legislation provides judicial protection of individual rights of everyone.

According to the petitions of citizens in violation of the Constitutional rights and freedoms and to inquiries of Courts, the Constitutional Court of the Russian Federation examines the validity of the law applied or subject to applying in the particular case.

On April 27, 1993, the Law of the Russian Federation "About the Appeal to the Court Against the Actions and decisions Violating the Rights and Freedoms of Citizens", was enacted according to which any individual may appeal to the Court against the actions of different bodies and officials, including the actions of the Regional Operator of Databank of Children or the Federal Operator of Databank of Children of the Russian Federation.

Any individual may appeal to the Court against the actions (inactions) if they violate the rights and freedoms of individuals (for example, the refusal to grant the permission to visit the child, the delayed direction of the release letter to the Regional Operator of Databank of Children for your Court hearing by the Federal Operator of Databank of Children, etc.).

Article 48

1. Everyone shall be guaranteed the right to have qualified legal assistance. Legal assistance shall be provided free of charge in cases specified by the Law.

2. Every person who has been detained, taken into custody or charged with a crime shall have the right to legal assistance (Defense Attorney) from the moment of, respectively, detention or indictment.

Commentary to article 48

Every individual has the right to count on the qualified legal assistance, which is guaranteed to him (her) by the Constitution. An individual may refer to the Bar Associations for legal assistance where qualified Attorneys work or to a law firm which has the applicable license to render legal services.

It is considered that the most qualified legal service is provided at Law firms where there are professional Attorneys who are members of the Bar Association and who have successfully passed the appropriate examinations and established the right to advocacy.

High demands are made of Attorneys. They shall have all-round knowledge, high moral and business qualities, and shall be able to advocate publicly the concern of the client while solving complicated legal problems and also shall have oratory skills.

Under the circumstances of political and economical instability in Russia it is very difficult to decide what kind of Lawyers it is possible to rely upon to solve the case and the family problems.

The system of advocacy in Russia differs considerably from the system in the USA. Lately in Russia, a number of companies and other law firms have appeared where the employees qualify themselves as Attorneys. However, under the current Russian Legislation, only a member of the Bar Association has the right to qualify himself or herself as an Attorney.

The activities of the Bar Association members are regulated under the Federal Law "About Attorneys Activities and Bar Associations in the Russian Federation", and the activities of other law firms and societies are not regulated under the Law. The Bar Associations make great demands of the members and control their activities.

Unlike Bar Associations, people working for law firms and societies, have similar sounding professional designations, and often do not have higher legal education. The Russian Law allows the registration of these firms, but does not invest them with the powers and does not place them under the duties, which the members of Bar Associations have.

Article 62

3. Foreign and stateless persons shall enjoy, in the Russian Federation, the rights of its citizens and bear their duties, except for the cases established by Federal Law or by the International Treaty of the Russian Federation.

Commentary to article 62

Persons who have evidence of their being the citizens of a foreign state are recognized as foreign citizens. Such evidence is a National Passport or a substituting document. The persons who have the partiality of a foreign state are also qualified as foreign citizens.

Stateless persons are the persons who are not Russian citizens and do not have the evidence of their being the citizens of a foreign state.

Foreign citizens and stateless persons have the same rights and duties as Russian citizens. Certain withdrawals may be established only by a Federal Act (for example, the specified persons have no elective franchises, or they may adopt the children whose information has been contained at the State Databank of Children without Parental Custody for not less than three months).

THE FAMILY CODE
OF THE RUSSIAN FEDERATION
(Excerpts)

December 29, 1995   # 223-FL

Enacted by the State Duma of December 8, 1995
Amendments were made effective November 15, 1997,
June 27, 1998 and January 2, 2000.

CHAPTER 18.

THE DETECTION AND PLACEMENT OF CHILDREN WHO HAVE BEEN LEFT WITHOUT PARENTAL CUSTODY.

Article 121. The protection of rights and interests of children who have been left without parental custody.

1. The protection of rights and interests of children is assigned to Bodies of Trusteeship and Guardianship in the event of the parents' death, or the removal of their parental rights, or the restriction of their parental rights, or the recognition of parents as incapable, or parents' illness, or parents' long absence, or parents' evasion of the child care or of the protection of their rights and interests, including the refusal of parents to take their children from educational institutions, medical institutions, establishments of the social protection of the population and other similar establishments, and also in other cases of the absence of parental custody.

Bodies of Trusteeship and Guardianship shall detect children who have been left without parental custody. They shall register such children and, proceeding from the merits of the loss of parental custody, choose the forms of placement for children who have been left without parental custody (article 123 of this Code), and also provide the post placement supervision of their living conditions, care and education.

The activities of entities and individuals other than Bodies of Trusteeship and Guardianship related to the detection and placement of children who have been left without parental custody are not allowed.

Commentary to article 121

The reasons for the loss by children of their parental custody may be different. The law cannot exhaustively express their list. Clause 1 of article 121 of the Family Code specifies only the most common of them. There may be apparent causes, and also the causes needed to be analyzed. The first include: the death of natural parents; their serious illness resulting in disability to take care of the child and to protect his (her) rights, the recognition of natural parents as incapable; the restriction or removal of the parental rights.

The rest of the reasons for the loss of parental custody which are listed in clause 1 of article 121 of the Family Code are the effects of the impossibility to protect the child and to take care of him (her) because of the custody of natural parents (in places of confinement, medical institutions, etc.), or the unwillingness to perform the parental duties. Though such unwillingness, in its turn, can be explained both by a non-motivated evasion of performing parental duties, and by the concatenation of circumstances (a new family, residing in another area, etc.), therefore, such causes shall be assessed.

Article 122. The detection and registration of children who have been left without parental custody.

1. The officials of different establishments (preschool educational institutions, general educational institutions, medical institutions and other related facilities) and other persons who have the information about the children, specified in clause 1 of article 121 of this Code are obligated to inform the Bodies of Trusteeship and Guardianship corresponding to the place where the children are actually present.

The Body of Trusteeship and Guardianship is obligated within three days after the date of receiving this information to conduct the study of the child's living conditions and, in case of fact-finding that there is the absence of parental custody or other relatives' care, to provide the protection of rights and interests of the child up to the decision about the placement of the child.

2. Heads of educational institutions, medical institutions, establishments of the social protection of the population and other similar establishments, in which there are children who have been left without parental custody, shall inform about the child, The Body of Trusteeship and Guardianship corresponding to the place where this establishment is situated within seven days after the day they knew, that the child may be placed with a family.

3. The Body of Trusteeship and Guardianship shall provide the placement of the child (article 123 of this Code) within a month after the date of receiving the information indicated in clauses 1 and 2 of this article. If it is impossible to place the

child with a family, it shall transmit the information about this child to the appropriate Body of Executive Power of the subject of the Russian Federation after the expiration of the given period.

Within a month after the date of receiving the information about the child, the Body of Executive Power of the subject of the Russian Federation shall organize his (her) placement in the family of citizens living within this subject of the Russian Federation. In the absence of such possibility it shall forward the said information to a Federal Body of Executive Power appointed by the Government of the Russian Federation, for registration in the State Databank of Children Without Parental Custody and for the ministration in the following placement of the child in the family of citizens of the Russian Federation residing within the Russian Federation.

The procedure of the formation and use of the State Databank of Children Without Parental Custody is defined by the Federal Law.

4. Heads of the orphanage institutions and officials of the authorities indicated in clauses 2 and 3 of this article shall be made accountable in the statutory order for the non-execution of their duties, provided by clauses 2 and 3 of this article, and for giving a certainly doubtful information, and also for other actions, directed at concealment of the child from placement in a family.

Commentary to article 122.

The commented article establishes the procedure of detecting children who have been left without parental custody, and also the order of their registration on the local level (Bodies of Trusteeship and Guardianship), Regional level (Regional Operator of the Databank of Children) and the Federal level (The Federal Operator of the Federal Databank of Children). The procedure of registration of such children is currently determined by the Federal Law "About the State Databank of Children without Parental Custody" dated April 16, 2001, # 44 FL the rules of keeping the State Databank of Children Without Parental Custody and it formation and use control dated April 4, 2002, # 217.

Section 2 of clause 1 of article 122 of the Family Code sets the rule, according to which Bodies of Trusteeship and Guardianship shall immediately (within three days) conduct the initial study after receiving the information about a child who has been left without parental custody. The purpose of such study is the verification of the received information (the acquaintance with the child and the study of his (her) living conditions). In case of fact-finding that there is the absence of parental custody, it is necessary to find his (her) relatives, who are able to provide the child with temporary care. Depending on the circumstances the child shall be immediately placed in an educational or medical institution or the establishment of the social protection of the population.

Currently the centralized registration of children who have been left without parental custody is assigned to the Regional and Federal Operators of the Databank of Children Without Parental Custody.

The Regional Operator forms the Regional Databank of Children on the grounds of the information about the children left without parental custody which has been transmitted from the Bodies of Trusteeship and Guardianship and realizes the registration of the children and organizes their placement for care in the families of citizens of the Russian Federation continuously residing within the Russian Federation.

The entry date of the information about the child left without parental custody in the Regional Databank of Children shall be the date when the Regional Operator receives the Child Questionnaire Form executed under the established procedure.

If the child left without parental custody has not been within the month following the entry date of the information about him (her) in the Regional Databank of Children placed for care with a family, the Regional Operator, within 3 days, transmits the copy of the Child Questionnaire Form and the photo of the child to the Federal Operator of the State Databank of Children (hereinafter known as the Federal Operator).

The Federal Operator forms the Federal Databank of Children on the ground of the information about the children left without parental custody which has been transmitted from the Regional Databanks of Children and realizes the registration of the children and promotes their placement for care in the families of citizens of the Russian Federation continuously residing within the Russian Federation.

The entry date of the information about a child who has been left without parental custody in the Federal Databank of Children shall be the date when the Federal Operator receives the copy of the Child Questionnaire Form.

The main purpose of children's registration is to help find a family for a child within the Russian Federation.

When it is impossible to place the child in a family for adoption or under trusteeship (guardianship) or a foster family, the child may be considered for adoption by foreigners, stateless persons or Russian citizens continuously residing outside the Russian Federation (except for the relatives of the child) after the expiration of three months following the date of the registration of the child in the State Databank of Children.

The officials of local authorities (Bodies of Trusteeship and Guardianship) and also of enforcement authorities of the subjects of the Russian Federation bear the administrative responsibility for the non-execution of their duties related to the detection and placement of children in the given period, specified by clause 3 of article 122 of the Family Code).

Article 123. The placement of children who have been left without parental custody.

1. Children who have been left without parental custody are subject to be placed in care with a family (for adoption, under trusteeship (guardianship) or in the foster family), and in the absence of such possibility in children's institutions for orphans or for children who have been left without parental custody, of all types (educational institutions, including children homes of a family type, medical institutions, establishments of the social protection of the population and other similar establishments).

The laws of the subjects of the Russian Federation may provide other forms of placement for children who have been left without parental custody.

The child's ethnic background, his (her) religious affiliation, native language, and the opportunity to provide continuity in education shall be considered in the placement of the child.

2. Up to the placement of children who have been left without parental custody in a family or in institutions specified in clause 1 of this article, the guardianship over children is temporarily assigned to the Bodies of Trusteeship and Guardianship.

Commentary to article 123

The Russian law gives the priority to the family care of children. The right of the child to live and be raised in a family is one of the fundamental rights of every child. Usually it is meant that the child is raised in the family of his (her) own parents. Concerning the children who have been left by any reason without parental custody, ensuring the right to be raised in a family means, that in choosing the forms of care for such children, Bodies of Trusteeship and Guardianship shall give the priority to the family forms of care (placement for adoption, under trusteeship (guardianship), and in a foster family).

Only in the cases when the placement of the child in a family is not obviously possible, children shall be placed in the appropriate institutions (depending on the age and health conditions) for the full State maintenance: the administration of these institutions exercises the rights and duties of the trustee (guardian) concerning the children, placed there. It is a temporary measure and steps for the search of a family for the child shall be ongoing.

CHAPTER 19

ADOPTION OF CHILDREN

Adoption is the preferable form of care for children who have been left without parental custody. Article 124 of the Family Code points to it directly (see commentary). The search of the fullest realization of interests of children, being placed for adoption is a very important social problem.

Adoption is a complicated legal institution. The fate of the child depends on the correct selection of the adoptive parent and the family, into which the child is placed. Mistakes in adoption may also violate the rights and interests of the child's parents and the adoptive parents as well. Therefore, the law regulates in detail the conditions and the order of the adoption procedure and of the annulment of adoption. Under the law effective prior to March 1, 1996, the process of adoption was simply an administrative procedure.

The new Family Code has established the legal procedure of the child adoption for the first time in the interests of children. The advantages of the legal procedure are obvious: the Court is independent and only obeys the law; it is unbound to any narrow departmental concerns. The Judge is professionally knowledgeable on the questions of law. The judicial (and not administrative) procedure of adoption exists in all civilized countries of the world. To adjust judicial proceedings, the amendments were also made to the Code of Civil Procedure of the Russian Federation of August 21, 1996.

Article 124. Children eligible for adoption.

1. Adoption is the priority form of the placement of children who have been left without parental custody.

2. Adoption is allowed in regard to children under 18 years of age and only in their interests pursuant to the requirements of paragraph 3 of clause 1 of article 123 of the present Code, and also considering the possibilities to provide children with a well-rounded, proper, physical, mental, intellectual and moral development.

3. The adoption of siblings by different persons is not allowed, except for the cases, when the adoption is in the best interests of the children.

4. The adoption of children by foreign citizens or stateless persons is allowed only in the cases, if it is obviously not possible to place these children with the families of citizens of the Russian Federation continuously residing within the Russian Federation, or for adoption to the relatives of the children irrespective of the citizenship and the place of residence of these relatives.

Children may be placed for adoption with the citizens of the Russian Federation continuously residing outside the Russian Federation, or with foreign citizens or stateless persons who are not the relatives of these children, after the expiration of three months following the date when the information about such children was received by the State Databank of Children Without Parental Custody as provided by clause 3 of article 122 of the present Code.

Commentary to article 124

While considering the case of adoption the law proceeds from a fundamental principle of the family legislation that is to safeguard the priority protection of the rights and interests of children under age. The observance of their interests is a compulsory condition of any adoption. The interests of the child in adoption are understood first of all as providing necessary conditions for his (her) well-rounded, proper, physical, mental and intellectual development.

Each child is a unique personality. Good care is not possible without knowing the child, his (her) abilities, instincts, inclinations, and hobbies. Obviously, each case of adoption is especially individual. The problem is to choose a family for the child, where his (her) interests will be realized in the best possible way; to take into account the features of his (her) character and mentality; to determine the psychological compatibility of the family and this particular child, etc.

At the same time the interests of the child on no account may be understood in a narrow sense, as providing satisfactory material security and housing conditions. It is not enough just to provide the child with good nutrition, clothes, and good conditions for his (her) activities and rest, though it is also very important. The main thing for the child is to constantly feel a favorable influence of the family, parental love, care, and caress; so that each child will develop as a cultured, versatile person, would receive education, and would be prepared for an active public life.

Only a person under 18 years of age may be adopted.

In the law, there is no direct requirement about the state of health of the children eligible for adoption. Implicitly provided, not only healthy children are subject to adoption, but also the children who have special medical conditions or developmental delays. No doubt, the raising of the child with special needs involves considerable difficulties, which in many cases, the birth parents are not able to overcome.

Therefore, adopters should be well informed about the child's state of health, and if the child has special needs they should be informed about the character of the illness and its possible consequences. For this purpose the child is examined by an expert medical board, which gives the conclusion about his (her) state of health, and also about the physical and mental development of the child. At the adopters' will, an independent medical examination of the child may be conducted. The permission to adopt the child with special needs may be granted, if it is determined that the adopter voluntarily and quite conscientiously takes the responsibilities for the care of the child.

Adoption is always voluntary. Therefore if there are no encumbrances for the placement of the child with a given person, the person himself (herself) decides, which particular child he (she) will adopt with the final solution of this problem in the interest of the child by the proper State Body. The adoption of two or more children at the same time is also possible.

In the interests of children, the article prescribes the rule, according to which the adoption of siblings by different persons is not allowed, since in case of adoption the legal relations shall stop not only between the child and his or her biological parents but with other relatives as well. The separation may be allowed as exception to the rule in those cases, when the children have never lived together, have never been

140

educated together and are not aware of each other and of their relationship, or one of them because of his (her) state of health is subject to custody in special medical and educational institutions, and also in other cases, when the adoption is in the best interests of this particular child.

The separation of children in case they were held in the same educational institution may be allowed only in the best interests of the child and provided that the adoptive parents do not insist on the preservation of the adoption privacy and are obliged not to interfere with the communication of the adopted child and his (her) siblings. The separation of siblings is possible as an exception if the children are placed for adoption simultaneously, but with the different families where they will acquire parents and a family.

As well as before, the Russian law allows the adoption of children, citizens of the Russian Federation by foreign citizens and stateless persons. Such adoption is granted on the general basis, though it is necessary to meet some additional requirements, provided by law. According to article 21 of the United Nations Convention relating to the rights of the child, which considers international adoption as the alternative way of child care, if the child cannot be placed in a family that is able to provide for his (her) care or adoption, and if providing of any appropriate care is not possible in the country of origin, article 124 of the Family Code gives the priority in adoption to the Russian citizens continuously residing within the Russian Federation. For this purpose there is the centralized registration of children who have been left without parental custody and who may be placed in the families of Russian citizens.

Foreigners and stateless persons may adopt Russian children only after the expiration of 3 months following the date of their registration in the State Databank of Children Without Parental Custody, irrespective of the age of children and their state of health. This adoption procedure also covers Russian citizens continuously residing outside Russia. The exception is made only for the child's relatives willing to adopt. They have the right to adopt the child on the general basis, like the Russian citizens, irrespective of their citizenship and place of residence.

The information about the children, registered in the State Databank, may be disclosed to foreign citizens only after the expiration of three months following the date of the child's registration and provided that these people are registered as prospective adoptive parents by a Regional or Federal Operator of the Databank of Children Without Parental Custody.

After the prospective adoptive parents are granted permission to visit the child, they shall have a personal meeting with the child, make a contact and inform the Regional Operator of the Databank of Children about their intent to adopt the child. This agency is then obligated within 10 days to send an inquiry letter to the Federal Operator of Databank of Children for the confirmation that the child has been placed in the State Databank of Children. In turn, the Federal Operator of Databank of Children, within 10 days after the date of receiving the inquiry letter shall send by special mail the verification letter that the child's information has been placed in the State Databank of Children for not less than three months and confirmation of impossibility of placing this child for custody in the family of the citizens of the Russian Federation continuously residing within the Russian Federation, or for the adoption by relatives of the child irrespective of the citizenship and place of residence of these relatives (commonly known as a release letter).

The adoption of children, citizens of Russia by foreign citizens is granted by a Regional Court.

Article 125. The procedure of adoption of a child

1. The Court, upon a petition of persons (person) who wish to adopt the child, executes an adoption proceeding. A hearing on the petition for granting the adoption is executed by the Court in a special procedure, according to the rules, prescribed by the legislation of civil procedure.

The Court considers cases related to the adoption in the presence of the adoptive parents, Bodies of Trusteeship and Guardianship and the Prosecutor.

2. For the entry of the Court decision of adoption, a Body of Trusteeship and Guardianship shall file, with the Court, the conclusion about the propriety of adoption and its compliance with the interests of the child being adopted and also the information about the personal contact of the adopters (adopter) and the child being adopted.

The procedure of the placement of children for adoption and also providing the supervision of the living conditions and care of children in the families of adoptive parents within the Russian Federation is determined by the Government of the Russian Federation.

3. The rights and obligations of the adoptive parents and the adopted child (article 137 of the present Code) are in effect from the date the Court decision goes into force.

The Court is obligated within three days after the effective date of the Court decision of adoption of the child to send an abstract of this Court decision to The Body of Civil State Registration corresponding to the place where the Court decision was granted.

The adoption of the child is subject to the state registration in the order prescribed for the State Civil State Registration.

Commentary to article 125

Adoption (from the legal point of view) is the establishment of legal relations (personal and property) between the adoptive parent (his (her) relatives) and the adopted child (his (her) issue), similar to those existing between natural parents and children (see article 137 of the Family Code and the commentary).

Adoption is granted judicially. Cases related to adoption are considered in a special procedure under the rules prescribed by the Code of Civil Procedure.

Adoption is a voluntary act, therefore cases related to adoption are instituted upon a petition of a person who wishes to adopt the child, and if a couple adopts the child, the case is instituted on their joint petition. When filing a petition the applicant is granted relief from paying the Court fee.

A petition for adoption shall meet general requirements related to the form and the contents of the petition, and also contain special data: the information about the adoptive parents, the children they wish to adopt, their natural parents, siblings; and the request for possible changes in the registration record concerning the birth of the adopted children. The Code of Civil Procedure of the Russian Federation determines a list of documents, which shall be filed with the Court, however; in addition, the Judge is entitled to request any other documents that are not specified by the law.

The documents filed with the Court, if given abroad, shall be certified by a notary and Apostilled. The documents are subject to translation into the Russian language. The translation shall be Notarially certified at the Consular Office of the Russian Federation in the country of residence of the adoptive parents or at a notary office within the Russian Federation.

The gravity of legal effects of the Court decision of adoption requires careful preparation of such cases. The Court decision of adoption is possible only after ascertaining that not only all legal conditions of adoption are observed, but also that the given adoption is in the best interests of the child. To reveal these essential circumstances, the Court, when preparing the case for hearing, obligates the Body of Trusteeship and Guardianship corresponding to the place of residence (actual presence) of the child to file with the Court, the Conclusion About the Propriety of Adoption and its compliance with the interests of the child together, with the report of living conditions and also the child's documents that are required for the Court decision of adoption: his (her) consent to adoption, if he (she) is 10 years of age or older, and the consent of his (her) parents, if it is required by the law.

The Court shall not schedule a hearing and consider the merits of the case until the Body of Trusteeship and Guardianship files with the Court the appropriate conclusion and the documents required for the solution of the case.

The indispensable evidence of the possibility to adopt the child for foreign citizens and also for stateless persons and the Russian citizens continuously residing outside Russia shall be the document verifying the registration of the adopted child in the State Databank of Children and the impossibility of his (her) placement in the family (for adoption, under guardianship or in the foster family) of the Russian citizens continuously residing within Russia, or for adoption with the relatives of the child irrespective of their citizenship and place of residence.

A Judge shall consider cases related to adoption not later than one month after the date when the preparation of the case for hearing is completed.

The petitioners are obligated to be present at the Court hearing. In addition, an Inspector of the Body of Trusteeship and Guardianship and the Prosecutor are also obligated to be present at the proceeding. This ensures the correct solution of cases of this category, which affect the essential rights and interests of children.

When it is necessary, other interested persons may be involved in the procedure: the natural parents of the child, his (her) relatives and the child himself (herself), if he (she) is 10 years of age or older.

The participants of the case relating to adoption (the Petitioner, Inspector of Bodies of Trusteeship and Guardianship, Prosecutor and other interested persons involved by the Court) are the persons participating in the procedure and have the appropriate procedural rights and responsibilities.

The reciprocal rights and obligations of the adoptive parents and the adopted children begin from the effective date of the Court decision but not from the date of the state registration of this fact in the Bodies of Civil State Registration.

Adoption is subject to the State registration in the Bodies of Civil State Registration corresponding to the place where the Court decision of adoption was granted. The registration is valuable for the protection of the rights and interests of the child. The registration reconfirms the fact of adoption. It also helps keep the privacy of adoption, as the new birth certificates are issued, where all the indispensable information (the name, patronymic name, and surname of the child, the information about his (her) parents etc.) must be written according to the Court decision of adoption.

To ensure the registration of adoption in time, the law establishes the responsibility for the Court, which rendered the Court decision of adoption, not later than 3 days after the Court decision is in force, to send an abstract of the Court decision to the corresponding Body of Civil State Registration.

Article 126. The registration of children eligible for adoption and persons who wish to adopt.

1. The registration of children eligible for adoption is effected in the order provided by clause 3 of article 122 of the present Code.

2. The registration of persons, who wish to adopt children, is effected in the order determined by the appropriate Body of Executive Power of subjects of the Russian Federation.

The registration of foreign citizens and stateless persons who wish to adopt children, citizens of the Russian Federation is effected by the Body of Executive Power of subjects of the Russian Federation or by a Federal Body of Executive Power (clause 3 of article 122 of the present Code).

Commentary to article 126

The order of the registration of children subject to adoption, and also of persons who wish to adopt children is regulated by the Federal Law "About The State Databank of Children without Parental Custody" dated April 16, 2001 and the Rules of Keeping the State Databank of Children Without Parental Custody and its formation and use control dated April 4, 2002.

Article 126.1. The inadmissibility of third party activities related to the adoption of children

1. The third party activities related to the adoption of children, defined as any activities of other persons with the intent to select and place children for adoption on behalf of and in the interests of persons who wish to adopt children, are not allowed.

2. Not relating to third party's adoption activities are the activities of Bodies of Trusteeship and Guardianship and Bodies of Executive Power executing the assigned obligations on detection and placement of children who have been left without parental custody, and also the activities of bodies specially authorized by foreign states, which are held within the Russian Federation under the International Treaty of the Russian Fed-

eration or on the basis of the principle of reciprocity. The organizations specified in this clause shall not pursue commercial purposes in their activities.

The Government of the Russian Federation upon the presentation of the Ministry of Justice of the Russian Federation and the Ministry of Foreign Affairs of the Russian Federation sets the procedure of activities for organizations of foreign states related to adoption of children within the Russian Federation and the procedure of their control.

3. The obligatory personal participation in the adoption procedure of persons (person) who wish to adopt the child does not divest them from having at the same time their legal representative, whose rights and obligations are determined by the civil and civil procedural legislation, and also from using the services of an interpreter if necessary.

4. The liability for conducting third party activities related to adoption of children is determined by the legislation of the Russian Federation.

Commentary to article 126.1

Only the bodies that are authorized by the state shall be engaged in the activities related to the selection of children and the placement of them for adoption.

These bodies are Bodies of Trusteeship and Guardianship, Bodies of Executive Power of the subjects of the Russian Federation, Regional and Federal Operators of the Databank of Children, and also adoption organizations specially authorized by foreign states.

According to the Constitution of the Russian Federation, each person has the right to receive qualified legal assistance of a professional Attorney, who is not just an Attorney, but also a member of a Bar Association.

Every person, citizen and non-citizen, has this right to have qualified legal assistance, which is guaranteed to him (her) by the Constitution. Citizens and non-citizens should refer to the Bar Associations for legal assistance where they will find qualified Attorneys.

It is considered that the most qualified legal service is provided at Law firms where there are professional Attorneys who have successfully passed the appropriate examinations and established the right to advocacy.

The obligatory personal participation of a person in the law proceeding does not exclude the participation of his (her) Attorney from the proceeding. Persons who cannot speak the Russian language, on which the Court procedure is conducted, are ensured the right to produce a statement, to give arguments and testimony, to appear before the Court and to present a petition in the native language, and also to use the services of an interpreter.

The adoption proceeding activities of any other persons are unlawful. Unauthorized third party adoption activities are subject to administrative or even criminal liability.

Thus, Article 5.37 of the Administrative Code of the Russian Federation provides that these illegal activities are liable to an administrative fine reaching from ten to twenty five times the minimum wages for citizens; and from forty to fifty times the minimum wages for government officials.

*If such actions are performed more than once or from prof-
it motives, then in accordance with article 154 of the Criminal
Code of the Russian Federation they shall be punished with a
fine from fifty to one hundred times the minimum wages or in
the amount of a nominal wage or other income of the convict-
ed person or with correctional labor for the term up to one
year or imprisonment for a term up to six months.*

Article 127. Persons who may adopt

1. Persons of either sex who are eighteen years of age or
older may be adoptive parents except for:

- persons recognized by Court as incapable or partially
capable;

- marital partners, if one of them is recognized by Court as
incapable or partially capable;

- persons having their parental rights removed by the
Court;

- persons disqualified by the Court from their responsibilities of guardian (the trustee) for inadequate execution of the
responsibilities assigned to them by the law;

- former adoptive parents, if a previous adoption was
annulled by the Court through their fault;

- persons, who cannot realize their parental rights due to
their state of health.

- persons, who at the moment of granting the adoption have no income providing for the adopted child the cost of living, determined in the subject of the Russian Federation where the adoptive parents (parent) live;

- persons who do not have a permanent place of residence, and also the living quarters meeting the established sanitary and technical requirements;

- persons having, at the moment of granting the adoption, a previous conviction for an intentional crime against the life or health of human beings.

2. Persons, who are not married to each other, cannot jointly adopt the same child.

3. If there are several persons wishing to adopt the same child, the priority right is granted to the relatives of the child provided that the requirements of clauses 1 and 2 of this article and the interests of the child being adopted are necessarily observed.

Article 128. The difference in age between the adoptive parent and child being adopted

1. The difference in age between the adoptive parent, who is not married, and the child being adopted should be not less than sixteen years. On the grounds recognized as a valid reason by the Court, the difference in age may be reduced.

2. When the child is adopted by the stepfather (stepmother), the difference in age specified by clause 1 of the present article is not required.

Commentary to articles 127 and 128

Adoption is allowed only in the interests of the child; therefore only persons who have the necessary parenting skills may be adoptive parents. According to article 127 of the Family Code persons of either sex who is of full age, that is 18 years of age or older may be adoptive parents though by virtue of emancipation they are also recognized as completely capable (article 27 of the Civil Code).

With intent to ensure the interests of children the Family Code increases the requirements to future adoptive parents. Such requirements were provided also by the previous legislation in force. Now the list has increased considerably.

Alongside the persons who have had their parental rights removed, incapable or partially capable, a married couple cannot adopt the child, if one of them is recognized by the Court as incapable or partially capable; persons, restricted by the Court in their parental rights; the former guardians, trustees and foster parents if they, through their fault, did not take proper care of the child, and also the persons who have medical conditions, not allowing them to take care of the child or endangering the child. The lists of illnesses are specified in the Government Regulation of the Russian Federation from May 1, 1996 # 542.

These diseases are: tuberculosis (fissile and chronic) of all forms of localization for patients of groups I, II, V of dispensary registration; diseases of viscera, the nervous system, ref-

erence-propulsion organs in the stage of decomposition; malignant oncology diseases of all forms of localization; drug addiction, toxicomania, alcoholism; infectious diseases; mental disorders; all diseases and traumas resulting in physical inability and eliminating capacity for work.

Besides, a definite difference in age is required between the adoptive parent (if he (she) is single) and the child being adopted. This difference should correspond to a usual difference in age between parents and children and ensure the normal family relations. According to article 128 of the Family Code a difference in age should be not less than 16 years.

If the stepfather (stepmother) or both marital partners adopt the child, the difference in age does not play any role. If there are valid grounds (the child looks upon the adoptive parent as the natural parent, the child is attached to the adoptive parent) the Court granting the adoption may allow adoption at a lesser difference in age between the child being adopted and the person who wishes to adopt.

The absence of statutory encumbrances to adoption does not mean that the person who has expressed the desire to become an adoptive parent is authorized to do that in all cases. As adoption is granted only under the Court decision and only in the interests of the child, a petition for adoption may be granted only at full conviction of the given body, that the adoption will meet the direct purposes. In the solution of the question about the admissibility of adoption in each concrete case, the personal qualities of the adoptive parents, the state of health, not only theirs, but also the state of health of their family members living together with them, the family relations, the relations between the family members and the child, and also the financial situation and housing conditions of the future adop-

tive parents, are taken into account. These circumstances are equally taken into account when both strangers and close relatives adopt a child.

The child may be adopted by a married couple or by a single person. As a result of adoption the child becomes a member of the family, the full value of which supposes both a father and mother for the child. Therefore it is desirable for adoption to be realized by a married couple (persons whose marriage is registered), or by the husband of the child's mother (stepfather), or the wife of the child's father (stepmother). The law also allows the adoption of the child by one spouse or a single person, a man or a woman. Single persons may be both relatives of the child or strangers. However, as against the previous law in force, the Family Code does not allow the adoption of the child by two persons who are not married.

Article 129. The parents' consent to the adoption of the child

1. The parents' consent to the adoption of the child is necessary. If the child's parents are under 16 years of age the consent of their parents or guardians (trustees) is also necessary, and in the absence of parents or guardians (trustees) the consent of a Body of Trusteeship and Guardianship is necessary.

The parents' consent to the adoption of the child shall be expressed in a written statement Notarially certified or certified by the head of the institution where a child who has been left without parental custody is held, or by a Body of Trusteeship and Guardianship corresponding to the place of the adoption proceeding or to the place of residence of the parents. It may also be expressed directly in the Court during the adoption proceeding.

2. The parents have the right to withdraw their consent to the adoption of the child before the Court rendered the Court decision of adoption.

3. The parents may express their consent to the adoption of the child by a particular person or without indicating a particular person. The parents' consent to the adoption of the child may be given only after his (her) birth.

Commentary to article 129

The right to personal care of the child is a major right of parents. Parental rights are granted to parents under the law, and the removal (restriction) of these rights is supposed only in statutory cases and in the established order. Thus, receiving the parents' consent to the adoption of their child is a major guarantee of ensuring their legitimate rights and one of the essential conditions of the adoption procedure.

If the child placed for adoption has parents, it is necessary to receive their consent to adoption. The law requires the consent of both parents, no matter whether they live together or not. One of them has no right to express the consent on behalf of the other. The refusal of one parent excludes the possibility of adoption and does not require reasoning and motivation. Possible cases of adoption of the child without the consent of parents or of one of them are specified by article 130 of the Family Code.

If the children placed for adoption have parents who are 16 years of age or older only their consent to adoption is required.

If the parents of the child being adopted are under 16 years of age, not only is their consent to the adoption of their child required, but also the consent of their legal representatives (parents, guardians or trustees), and in their absence the consent of the Body of Trusteeship and Guardianship is required.

The parents' consent shall be expressed in writing; it shall be clearly formulated and certified by a notary or Bodies of Trusteeship and Guardianship, or the head of the children's institution, in which the child is held.

The consent to adoption may be expressed by the parent (parents) directly in the Court of the adoption proceeding (it is incorporated in the record of the Court hearing and is indicated in the Court decision).

Since the natural parents lose all of their rights and are released from the obligations in respect to their children only after granting the adoption, they have the right at any time up to the moment of the rendering of the Court decision of adoption to withdraw their consent, given before. They are not obligated to explain motives, according to which they have decided to withdraw the consent.

The parents' consent to the adoption of their child may be of two kinds:

- The consent that the child shall be adopted by a particular person, a specific consent to adoption;

- The consent to adoption without indicating a particular adoptive parent, a general consent. In these cases, in the interests of the child, the right to choose the adoptive parent belongs to the Regional/Federal Operator of the Databank of Children.

For the purpose of ensuring the child's rights and interests and preventing child trade, Bodies of Trusteeship and Guardianship shall conduct a study and give their conclusion about the conformity of the adoption to the interests of the child.

Article 130. The adoption of the child without the parents' consent

The parents' consent to the adoption of their child is not required in cases:

- if they are unknown or recognized by the Court as missing;

- if they are recognized by the Court as incapable;

- if the parental rights are removed by the Court (under the observance of the requirements of clause 6 of Article 71 of the present Code);

- on the grounds recognized by the Court as invalid, if they do not live together with the child for more than six months and evade providing care and maintenance for the child.

Commentary to article 130

In order to adopt the child it is necessary to receive the consent of his (her) parents, which by operation of law is a compulsory condition for adoption. Article 130 of the Family Code provides contingent restrictions of this general rule. The list of circumstances, established by the given article, with the existence of which the adoption of children is allowed without their parents' consent, is comprehensive and is not subject to extensive interpretation.

To prove these circumstances, there shall be the documents that confirm them.

Children may be placed for adoption without their parents consent if the parents are unknown (for example, if the exposed children are adopted), or recognized by Court as missing or incapable. Irrespective of the will of the parents, the adoption of children is also granted, when their parents have their parental rights removed. However, adoption in these cases is possible only after the expiration of 6 months following the date of entering the judgment about the removal of their parental rights (Article 71, Clause 6 of the Family Code).

The law also provides the possibility of adoption without the parents' consent in cases when they evade providing their child with care and maintenance. It is allowed only if all of the conditions established in article 130 of the Family Code are satisfied:

- living apart from the child for more than 6 months;

- evasion of providing the child with care and maintenance;

- the absence of valid reasons of such conduct (for example: an illness, a long business trip);

- encumbrances on the part of the other parent related to the communication with the child, etc.

If there is not at least one of these conditions, adoption without the natural parents consent to the adoption is not allowed.

Article 131.   The consent to adoption of the guardians (trustees), foster parents, and heads of the institutions, in which children who have been left without parental custody, is held.

1. The written consent to adoption on the part of the guardians (trustees) is necessary for the adoption of children who are under guardianship (trusteeship).

The written consent to adoption on the part of the foster parents is required for the adoption of children who are in foster families.

The written consent to adoption on the part of the heads of the institutions is required for the adoption of children who have been left without parental custody and are held in educational institutions, medical institutions, institutions of social protection of the population and other similar institutions.

2. In the interests of children, the Court is entitled to render the Court decision of adoption without the consent of persons indicated in clause 1 of the present article.

Commentary to article 131

If the child is under guardianship (trusteeship), or in a foster family, the consent to adoption on the part of the child's guardian (trustee), or his (her) foster parents is required. If the child is held in a children's institution, it is necessary to receive the consent to adoption on the part of the administration of this institution, which is assigned, according to the law, the responsibilities of the guardian (trustee) concerning the children placed in these institutions. The consent shall be expressed in writing.

Receiving the consent to adoption from the persons specified in clause 1 of the commented article does not exclude the necessity of receiving the consent from the child's parents if they are alive and are not recognized by Court as incapable or missing, and have their parental rights removed, and also if they do not evade providing the child with care and maintenance.

If the guardian (trustee) or the foster parents or the administration of a children's institution refuse to give their consent to the adoption of the child, the Court is entitled to render the Court decision of adoption without their consent, proceeding only from the interests of the child. According to the law, the adoption of the child is the basis for the release of the guardian (trustee) from his responsibilities, and also for the advance avoidance of the agreement about the child's living in a foster family.

Article 132. The consent of the child being adopted to the adoption

1. In order to adopt the child who is 10 years of age or older, his (her) consent to adoption is necessary.

2. If before filing a petition for adoption the child had lived in the family of the adoptive parent and considers the adopter his (her) parent, the adoption, as an exception, may be granted without the consent of the child being adopted.

Commentary to article 132

Receiving the consent to adoption from the child who is 10 years of age or older is a compulsory condition for adoption. The consent shall be expressed in any written form.

Clause 2 of the commented article provides a contingent exception to the general rule established by clause 1. Its meaning is as follows: The formal consent is not required when the child, under 10 years of age, had lived in the family of the adoptive parent and considers the adopter his (her) parent. To insist on the formal consent under such circumstances means to disclose the secret of adoption. The consent of the child in these cases is confirmed by his (her) entire life situation, and that shall be noted and certified in the inspection certificate of his (her) living conditions.

Article 133. The consent of the adopter's spouse to the adoption of the child

1. If one spouse adopts the child, the consent of the other spouse to adoption is required if the child is not adopted by both of them.

2. The consent of the spouse to the adoption of the child is not required if the marital partners have ceased their family relations and have not lived together for more than one year, and the place of residence of the other spouse is unknown.

Commentary to article 133

The preferable form of adoption is the adoption of the child by the marital partners jointly. In this case the position of the child in the family comes most closely to the position of the natural children. The adoption of the child by only one spouse is less desirable. It may be allowed, if under given specific circumstances it will be in the interests of the child.

If, by virtue of different reasons, one of the marital partners does not wish to become the adoptive parent, though he (she) does not object to the adoption of the child by the other spouse, then receiving the consent of the adopter's spouse according to article 133 of the Family Code is a compulsory condition to adoption. Receiving this consent is necessary first of all in the interests of the adoptee, since it is impossible to hope for normal living conditions of the child in the family, if the adopter's spouse objects to adoption.

For the purpose of ensuring the child's interests the consent of the spouse is not required, if it is determined, that the marital partners have actually ceased their family relations and have not lived together for more than one year, and the place of residence of the other spouse is unknown.

Article 134. The name, patronymic name and surname of the adopted child

1. The adopted child reserves his (her) name, patronymic name and surname.

2. At the request of the adoptive parent the adopted child is given the surname of the adoptive parent, and also the stated name. The patronymic name of the adopted child is determined according to the name of the adoptive parent, if the adoptive parent is a man, and if the child is adopted by a woman, the patronymic name is determined according to the name of the person stated as the father of the adopted child. If the surnames of the adoptive parents are different, the adopted child is given the surname of one of them under their mutual agreement.

3. If the child is adopted by a single person: at his (her) request, the surname, name and patronymic name of the mother (father) of the adopted child are recorded in the book of birth records as stated by this person (adoptive parent).

4. The surname, name and patronymic name of the adopted child who is ten years of age or older may be changed only with his (her) consent, except for the cases, specified by clause 2 of article 132 of the present Code.

5. The change of the surname, name and patronymic name of the adopted child shall be included in the Court decision of adoption.

Commentary to article 134

At the request of the adoptive parents, the child's surname and name may be changed. Usually this request is caused by the desire to save the privacy of adoption. If the child is ten years of age or older, his (her) consent to the change of the name is compulsory.

When the adoptive parents have different surnames, the surname of the adopted child may be changed only to a surname of one of them chosen under their agreement.

If a single woman adopts the child he (she) is also given her surname at her request. As for the information about the father, it is recorded in this case according to the words of the adoptive mother, and the child is given the surname of the adoptive mother, and the name and patronymic name as stated by the adoptive mother. The same rights are granted to the adopter who is a single man.

Under the Court decision of adoption (with including in the Court decision the change of the surname, name and patronymic name of the adopted child), which is transmitted to a Body of Civil State Registration, the corresponding changes are incorporated in the child's birth record and the new certificate of birth is issued.

Article 135. The change of the date and place of birth of the adopted child

1. To ensure the privacy of adoption the date of birth of the adopted child may be changed at the request of the adoptive parent, but not more than to three months, his (her) birthplace may also be changed.

The change of the date of birth of the adopted child is allowed only if the adopted child is less than one year of age.

2. The change of the date and place of birth of the adopted child shall be incorporated in the Court decision of adoption.

Commentary to article 135

The date of birth may be changed not more than 3 months, only for the purpose of keeping the privacy of adoption, i.e. the date of birth of the adoptee may be recorded within the limits of 3 months earlier or later than his (her) actual birth. The previous law in force allowed the change of the date of birth within the limits of half a year. It is possible only if the adopted child is under one year of age. The law previously in force did not provide this restriction.

Under the Court decision of adoption Bodies of Civil State Registration shall enter the corresponding changes in the birth record of the child and issue the new certificate of his (her) birth.

Article 136. Recording the adopters as the parents of the adopted child

1. At the request of the adoptive parents the Court may render a judgment about recording the adopters in the book of birth records as the parents of their adopted child.

2. This record relating to the adopted child may be incorporated if the adopted child, who is 10 years of age or older, has given his (her) consent, except for the cases specified by clause 2 of article 132 of the present Code.

3. The Court decision of adoption shall state the necessity of entering this record.

Commentary to article 136

The creation of real family relations, based on mutual love, respect, and attachment, is easier, if the child feels itself a full-fledged member of the adoptive family. With the purpose of the best possible equality of the adopted children with natural children, the law provides conditions, under which the adopters are recorded as the parents of the adopted child.

Proceeding from the interests of the child and specific circumstances, the Court renders a judgment recording the adopters as the parents of the adopted child. If the child is 10 years of age or older, his (her) consent is compulsory. In cases, when the child has lived in the family of the adopter and considers the adopter his (her) parent, the consent of the child is not required.

Article 137. Legal effects of the adoption of the child

1. The adopted children and their issue in relation to the adoptive parents and their relatives, and the adoptive parents and their relatives in relation to the adopted children and their issue shall stand equal in personal non-property and property rights and obligations to the relatives by origin.

2. The adopted children shall lose personal non-property and property rights and be released from the obligations in relation to their natural parents (relatives).

Article 138. The reservation of the adopted child's right to pension and benefits.

The child who, up to the moment of the adoption, has had the right to pension and benefits, prescribed to him because of the parents' death, reserves this right in case of adoption.

Commentary to articles 137 and 138

The adoption is not only the form of placing children for care in a family, but it is also a juridical fact having legal effects. Children acquire not only new parents, but also other relatives. Therefore, the law prohibits marriages between the adoptive parents and the adoptees. From the moment of adoption there arise the same rights and obligations, which are provided in relation to natural parents and children.

By implication of law, the adoptive parents are, first of all, entitled to parental rights and obligations, which the natural parents forfeit. The requirement of the law that obligates parents to raise their children, to take care of their health, and their physical, mental, intellectual and moral development fully refers to the adoptive parents who voluntarily take the responsibilities to take care of the adopted child.

The adoptive parents, as well as the natural parents, are obligated to endow their adopted children.

In turn, the adopted children are obligated to take care of and to help their adoptive parents. The support of their incapable adoptive parents, requiring help, is the obligation of the adult employable adopted children. The fact that the adoption is not a secret for the adoptee or the adopters has no legal effect.

The adoptee and also the adoptive parent (and his (her) relatives) acquires, as a result of adoption, not only the rights and obligations arising from the family relations, but also all those rights and obligations, which are provided by standards of other branches of the legislation, and one of the grounds of acquiring such rights and obligations is the fact of the family relationship. So, according to the standards of the succession law at hereditary succession, the adopted children in relation to the adoptive parents, and the adoptive parents in relation to the adopted children are the apparent heirs.

The adoptive parents, being the legal representatives of the non-adult adopted children, make civil bargains on behalf of the children who are under 14 years of age (minors), or agree to bargains by the children who are from 14 till 18 years of age. The adoptive parents are responsible for harm inflicted by a minor under 14 years of age, and also bear the secondary (additional) liability for harm inflicted by the children who are from 14 till 18 years of age, if the children do not have their own income or other assets, sufficient for indemnification of harm.

Under the general rule, legal relations between the adopted child and the natural parents cease from the moment of the adoption of the child.

Article 139. The privacy of adoption

1. The privacy of the adoption of the child is protected by the law.

The Judges who have rendered the Court decision of the adoption of the child or the officials who have carried out the state registration of this adoption, and also the persons otherwise informed about the adoption of the child are obligated to keep the privacy of adoption.

2. The persons specified in clause 1 of the present article, who have disclosed the privacy of the adoption of the child against the will of his (her) adoptive parents, are made accountable in the statutory order.

Commentary to article 139

The Constitution of the Russian Federation recognizes and ensures the right of citizens to personal and family privacy. The information about adoption may be considered both as family and personal privacy. Specific measures relating to the realization of the right of citizens to the privacy of adoption are provided in article 139 of the Family Code and in some other articles of chapter 19 of the Family Code.

Beyond doubt, creating for the child in the adoptive family such conditions for living and upbringing that, to a great extent, are similar to the conditions of raising natural children is much easier, if the child considers the adoptive parents his (her) natural parents. With the purpose of ensuring the privacy of adoption the law provides the possibility of changing at the request of the adoptive parent the name, patronymic name and surname of the adopted child, recording the adopters as his (her) parents, and also the possibility of changing the date and place of birth of the adopted child.

However, the privacy of adoption is not a mandatory element of any adoption. Moreover, in some cases the adoption is not a secret for the adoptee (when the adopted children remember their parents, and also for the children who are 10 years of age or older, because under the law their consent to adoption is compulsory, see article 132 of the Family Code and the commentary). In the cases, when at the moment of adoption the child through the age or by other reasons could not know about the fact of adoption, the law binds further keeping the privacy of adoption only with the will of the adoptive parents. For some reasons, including pedagogical considerations, the adoptive parent may find it rational to inform the child, that he (she) has been adopted. However, even in these cases the fact of adoption cannot be disclosed to other persons without the consent of the adoptive parent.

According to the law protecting the privacy of adoption (i.e. the information about the fact of adoption, which the adoptive parent does not think proper to disclose to anyone) is the obligation of all the officials participating in the Court decision or in its subsequent registration, and also of other persons informed about the adoption. Any certificates or other case papers may be given to the adoptive parent, and they may be given to other persons only with his (her) consent or after demand of judicial and investigative bodies.

Protecting the fact of adoption secret depends, as it has already been mentioned, on the will of the adoptive parent. The disclosure of this fact to somebody is allowed only with the consent of the adoptive parent. Persons, who have disclosed the privacy of adoption against the will of the adoptive parent, are criminally liable. According to article 155 of the Criminal Code, criminal liability is provided for the disclosure of the privacy of adoption.

Article 140. The annulment of adoption

1. The annulment of adoption of the child is granted judicially.

2. A case of the annulment of adoption is considered with the participation of a Body of Trusteeship and Guardianship, and also the Prosecutor.

3. The adoption ends up from the effective date of a Court decision of the annulment of adoption.

The Court is obligated within three days after the effective date of the Court decision of the annulment of adoption to send an abstract of this Court decision to the Body of Civil State Registration corresponding to the place where the Court decision of annulment was granted.

Commentary to article 140

The ground of the termination of adoption is a Court decision of the annulment of adoption. The legal proceeding relating to the annulment of adoption is granted by the Court as action proceeding according to the rules established by the Code of Civil Procedure. The period of limitation of action for the claim of the annulment of adoption is not established.

Cases of the annulment of adoption fall into the category of disputes connected with the raising of children. Therefore, irrespective of the fact of who enters the claim of the annulment of adoption, a Body of Trusteeship and Guardianship shall be involved in the proceeding. The Body of Trusteeship and Guardianship is obligated to conduct the study of living conditions of the adopted child and to submit to the Court the conclusion based on the issue.

A Court decision of the annulment of adoption has no retroactive effect and terminates the adoption relations only for the future. An adoption is recognized as terminated after the effective date of the Court decision.

After a Court decision of the annulment of adoption is rendered, an abstract (or a copy) of the Court decision shall be transmitted by the Court to the Body of Civil State Registration, in which the registration of the adoption was effected.

If an adoption is annulled, the Body of Civil State Registration includes the corresponding notes in the record of adoption and restores in the birth record of the child the information about his (her) parents. The surname, name and patronymic name of the child are recorded according to the Court decision.

Article 141. The grounds of the annulment of adoption

1. The adoption of the child may be annulled in cases, if the adoptive parents evade performing the duties of parents, assigned to them, abuse their parental rights, are cruel to their adopted child, or are alcohol or drugs addicts.

2. The Court is entitled to annul an adoption also on other grounds proceeding from the interests of the child and taking into account the opinion of the child.

Commentary to article 141

The family legislation proceeds from the principle of indissolubility of the adoption relations. When the Court decision of adoption is rendered, it is supposed that the relations have been established forever. The annulment of adoption can creates great harm to the child, and strongly affects his (her) interests. Therefore, the law consequently ensures stability of adoption, both in the procedure of adoption and in its annulment. The possibility of the annulment of adoption is allowed only when the adoption stops functioning, i.e. when the living conditions and care of the child, which have been created as a result of adoption, do not meet his (her) interests.

The law assigns to the adoptive parents the same responsibilities of care that are assigned to natural parents of the child. They are obligated to raise the adopted children, to care of their health, physical, mental, intellectual and moral development, to protect their interests, and to endow the children. Therefore, those circumstances that are the grounds of the removal of the parental rights are the unconditional grounds of the annulment of adoption. If the conduct of the parents offen-

sive against the interests of the child is determined, the Court renders the Court decision of the annulment of adoption. In these cases the consent of the child to the annulment of adoption is not required.

Adoption, as well as family relations established pursuant to the law may be annulled not only if offensive conduct of the adoptive parents is determined, but also if there are other grounds, if by force of circumstances (both depending or not depending on the adoptive parent) it was not possible to create the required family relations. This very rule is established by clause 2 of the commented article, according to which the cause of claiming the annulment of adoption may be any circumstances affecting the interests of the child.

The process of raising children is rather hard. It requires special relationships between the child and the person raising him (her). Sometimes depending on the personal qualities of the child or the adoptive parent there develops such relations between them, with which the child feels like a stranger in the family. If for some reason, between the child and the adoptive parent, the relations of love, confidence, respect etc have not been created, there are no reasons to hope for the improvement of these relations in the future. The continuation of adoption in such cases would contradict the purposes of adoption.

The annulment of adoption may be caused by objective reasons, in particular: the objective failure of the adoptive parent to perform his (her) duties (a serious illness, a considerable change in family circumstances, etc.), the rise of circumstances, connected with the personality of the child (a severe incurable disease, revealed after his (her) adoption, etc.), changing of circumstances after the adoption, which are significant for the child (the recovery of the severely sick parents, to whom the child was bound to and whom the child cannot forget after adoption, the restoration of their active capacity, etc.).

The circumstances that cause the necessity of the annulment in the interests of the adopted child are so diverse that the law does not provide a comprehensive list. In each specific case the Court proceeds taking into account all the circumstances of the case, in the interests of the child.

Article 142. Persons entitled to claim the annulment of adoption

Persons entitled to claim the annulment of adoption are the child's natural parents, the adoptive parents of the child, the adopted child who is fourteen years of age or older, a Body of Trusteeship and Guardianship, and also the Prosecutor.

Commentary to article 142

Not only Bodies of Trusteeship and Guardianship and the Prosecutor, but also the adoptive parents of the child, his (her) natural parents, and the adopted child, if he/she is 14 years of age or older, are entitled to claim the annulment of adoption.

If other persons, who are not specified in the commented article, think that the adoption is not in the interests of the child, these persons (the relatives of the child or other citizens, state or public organizations) have the right to inform the Bodies of Trusteeship and Guardianship or to address the Prosecutor, who shall make a decision about initiating the Court proceedings.

Article 143. The effects of the annulment of adoption

1. After the adoption of the child is annulled by the Court, the mutual rights and obligations of the adopted child and the adoptive parents (the relatives of the adoptive parents) shall cease and the mutual rights and obligations of the child and his (her) natural parents (his (her) relatives) shall be re-established, if it is required in the best interests of the child.

2. After the adoption is annulled, the child, according to the Court decision, is placed with the natural parents. In the absence of the natural parents, and also if the placement of the child with the parents is not in his (her) interests, the child is placed into custody of a Body of Trusteeship and Guardianship.

3. The Court also solves the problem, whether to reserve the child's name, patronymic name and surname given to him in connection with his (her) adoption. The change of the name, patronymic name or surname of the child who is ten years of age or older is possible only with his (her) consent.

4. The Court proceeding from the interests of the child is entitled to oblige the former adoptive parent to pay money for child maintenance.

Commentary to article 143

On the ground of a Court decision of the annulment of adoption under the general rule, all legal relations between the adopted child, on the one hand, and the adoptive parent and his (her) relatives, on the other hand, shall cease, and the rights and obligations between the child and his (her) natural parents and other relatives shall be re-established. The annulment of adoption does not cause automatic re-establishment of legal relations between the child and his (her) parents (relatives). The decision of this question is held depending on the interests of the child. It concerns those cases, when in general or at the moment of the annulment of adoption, it is not obviously possible to re-establish legal relations between the child and his (her) natural parents (for example, the parents are missing, are disqualified from their parental rights, do not wish to raise the child, etc.).

If the Court comes to the conclusion, that such re-establishment is possible, it shall specify it in the Court decision. Legal relations, lost between the child and his (her) other relatives by virtue of adoption are re-established simultaneously.

If the adoption is annulled according to clause 2 of article 143 of the Family Code, the Court in all cases determines the further destiny of the child. It shall be specified in the Court decision who the child shall be placed with, the parents or in custody of Bodies of Trusteeship and Guardianship, which according to the law shall determine the form of placement of the child after the annulment of his (her) adoption.

After the annulment of adoption, the rights and obligations that have arisen as a result of adoption shall cease only for the future after the annulment of adoption time. The previous legal relations are not recognized as invalid, i.e. that they did not exist. Therefore, after the annulment of adoption, some rights of the adopted child and obligations of the adoptive parent may be reserved.

If the adoption of the child is annulled, the Court has the right, if it finds it necessary in the interests of the child, to reserve the name, patronymic name and surname given to him in connection with his (her) adoption. If the child is 10 years of age or older, his (her) desire is taken into account. Therefore, while considering the question about the annulment of adoption the Court is obligated at the same time to deliver a judgment, not only about the placement of the child, but also, whether to reserve the name, patronymic name and surname of the child given to him/her as a result of adoption. The absence of such directions makes difficult the consequent registration of the annulment of adoption in Bodies of Civil State Registration.

Clause 4 of the commented article establishes one more essential exception to the general rule about the termination of all legal relations between the adopted child and the adoptive parent: it is the right of the Court to oblige the former adoptive parent to pay money for the maintenance of the child. By implication of the law, this question is determined at the discretion of Court, depending on the specific circumstances of the case, irrespective of the cause, by virtue of which the adoption is abrogated. As the collection of child support is not a measure of the responsibility of the adoptive parents, but the means of protection of children's interests, it seems, that at the heart of the decision about collecting child support for the child's maintenance there shall be the neediness of it by the child.

The reservation of the right of the adopted child to receiving the appropriate child support, and the amount of child support shall be necessarily specified in the Court decision of the annulment of adoption.

Article 144. The inadmissibility of the annulment of adoption after the adopted child has attained lawful age

The annulment of adoption is not allowed, if to the moment of claiming the annulment of adoption the adopted child has attained lawful age, except for the cases, when for such annulment there is a mutual consent of the adoptive parent and the adopted child, and also the natural parents of the adopted child, if they are alive, and have not had their parental rights removed or not recognized by Court as incapable.

Commentary to article 144

After attainment by the adopted child of lawful age, the adoption may be annulled only with the consent of the adoptive parent and the adoptee and his (her) natural parents. The consensus of these persons is the independent cause for the annulment of adoption by Court at their request. If at least one of these persons objects, the annulment of adoption after attainment by the adoptee of lawful age, is not allowed. In cases, where the parents have died, were in due Courts (when the child was a minor) had their parental rights removed or was recognized by Court as incapable, the annulment of adoption is granted by the Court if there is a mutual consent of the adoptive parent and the adult adopted child to the termination of the adoption relations.

THE CODE OF CIVIL PROCEDURE OF THE RUSSIAN FEDERATION
(Excerpts)

The last amendments made on August 7, 2000

Chapter 29.1. THE ADOPTION OF THE CHILD

(This chapter was enacted by Federal Law
on August 21, 1996, # 124-FL)

Article 263.1. Filing a petition for adoption

The citizens of the Russian Federation who wish to adopt the child shall file a petition for the adoption of the child with a District Court according to the place of residence of the child being adopted.

The citizens of the Russian Federation residing continuously outside the Russian Federation, or foreign citizens, or stateless persons wishing to adopt the child, who is a citizen of the Russian Federation, shall file a petition for the adoption of the child with a Regional Court according to the place of residence of the child being adopted. *(Amended on June 25, 1998 # 90-FL)*

Commentary to article 263.1

The legal procedure of adoption was first established in the Russian Legislation by the Family Code of the Russian Federation. However, this procedure had not been applied until the

Code of Civil Procedure was amended. The legal procedure of adoption has been applied since September 27, 1996.

Before that, there was an administrative procedure. The citizens of Russia and foreign citizens applied to the administrative bodies of a region.

The establishment of the legal procedure of adoption can be explained by a number of reasons, first of all, by the fact that with the administrative procedure there were the gross violations of the current legislation related to the solution of adoption problems, and also by the fact, that in most foreign countries adoption is granted judicially, and it guarantees, to a considerable degree, the protection of the rights of children and the adoptive parents.

From September 1996 until June 1998 all the cases related to adoption were considered by District Courts according to the place of residence of the child. Currently, if the adoptive parents are citizens of the Russian Federation residing continuously outside of the Russian Federation or foreign citizens, or stateless persons, the case is considered by a Regional Court (which is a more superior body in relation to a District Court).

Despite the legal procedure, which exists at present, some powers still belong to the Bodies of District Administration (Bodies of Executive Power): organizing the registration of children who have been left without parental custody, the registration of persons who wish to adopt children, the preparation of reports about the expediency of adoption by particular persons, etc.

Article 263.2. The contents of a petition

A petition for the adoption of the child shall contain the following information:

1) The surnames, names, and patronymic names of the adoptive parents (parent), and their place of residence;

2) The surname, name, patronymic name and date of birth of the adopted child, the place of his (her) residence (presence), the information about the natural parents of the adopted child and his (her) siblings;

3) The circumstances justifying the request of the adoptive parents (parent) for the adoption of the child, and the evidence confirming these circumstances;

4) The request for the change of a surname, name, and patronymic name of the adopted child, his (her) date of birth (if the adopted child is under one year of age), the birthplace of the adopted child, the request for recording the adoptive parents (parent) as the parents (parent) in the child's birth record. At the will of the adoptive parents (parent) the corresponding changes are rendered in the birth record of the child.

The following documents shall be filed together with a petition for adoption:

1) A copy of the birth certificate of the adoptive parent, if the adoptive parent is single;

2) A copy of the marriage certificate of the adoptive parents (parent), if the adoptive parents (parent) are married;

3) The consent to adoption of the spouse, if the child is adopted by one of the marital partners, or the document confirming that the marital partners have stopped their family relations and haven't been living together for more than one year, and the place of residence of the spouse is unknown. If it is impossible to add the appropriate document to the petition for adoption, the petition shall specify the evidence confirming these facts;

4) A medical report about the state of health of the adoptive parents (parent);

5) A verified statement from the employer about the job position and wages or a copy of the income tax return or other documents verifying the income;

6) The document confirming the right to use the living quarters or the proof of home ownership;

7) If the child who is a citizen of the Russian Federation, is adopted by the citizens of the Russian Federation residing continuously outside the Russian Federation, or by foreign citizens or stateless persons, the documents specified in clauses 1-6 of part 2 of the present article are required, and also the Homestudy report made by a specially authorized organization of the country of citizenship of the adoptive parents (or of the country of permanent residence if the child is adopted by stateless persons) about their living conditions and the possibility to be the adoptive parents; the permission for entry and permanent residence given to the adopted child by an authorized body of the appropriate State;

8) If the child who is a foreign citizen is adopted by the citizens of the Russian Federation within the territory of the Russian Federation, the documents specified in clauses 1-6 of part 2 of the present article are required, and also the consent to adoption given by the legal representative of the child and by a authorized body of the country of citizenship of the child, and, if it is required according to the legislation of the said country and (or) under the International Treaty of the Russian Federation, the consent of the child to adoption. (*Amended on June 25, 1998 # 90-FL*)

Commentary to article 263.2

The article particularizes the contents of a petition for adoption, which is filed by petitioners with the Court. Besides, the article contains the list of the required documents, which a petitioner shall file together with the petition. The petitioner himself (herself) shall collect these documents.

The Judge is entitled to request additional documents or evidence.

The documents of the adoptive parents residing in other countries shall be legalized in the statutory order. It means that all the documents shall be certified by a notary of the country, where the documents have been made, and shall be affixed with the Apostille of the country (State). After the legalization, the documents shall be translated into Russian, and the translation shall be Notarially certified at the Russian consular office within the country of residence of the adoptive parent or by a notary within the Russian Federation.

Article 263.3. The action of the Judge after a petition for adoption has been filed

The Judge, while preparing a case for the Court proceeding, obligates the Bodies of Trusteeship and Guardianship, corresponding to the place of residence of the child being adopted, to present to the Court the report about the propriety and compliance of the adoption with the interests of the child being adopted.

The following documents shall be added to the report of a Body of Trusteeship and Guardianship:

1. The report on the examination of living conditions of the adoptive parents (parent) made by a Body of Trusteeship and Guardianship corresponding to the place of residence (presence) of the child being adopted or to the place of residence of the adoptive parents (parent);

2. The birth certificate of the adopted child;

3. A medical report on the state of health, and physical and mental development of the child being adopted;

4. The consent of the child being adopted, who is ten years of age or older, to adoption, and also to possible changes in his (her) name, patronymic name, and surname and to recording the adoptive parents (parent) as his (her) parents (except for the cases, when such consent is not required under the law);

5. The consent of the parents of the child to his (her) adoption (and if the parents of the child being adopted are under sixteen years of age, the consent of their legal representatives, and in their absence, the consent of a Body of Trusteeship and Guardianship) or the document confirming the presence of a condition, under which in accordance with article 130 of the Family Code of the Russian Federation the adoption of the child is allowed without the consent of his (her) parents;

6. The consent to adoption of the child's guardian (trustee), the foster parents or the head of the institution, in which a child who has been left without parental custody is being held;

7. If the child is adopted by the citizens of the Russian Federation residing continuously outside the Russian Federation, or by foreign citizens or stateless persons who are not the relatives of the child, it is necessary to present the document confirming the availability of the information about the child being adopted in the State Databank of Children Without Parental Custody, and also the documents that confirm that the child's information has been placed in the State Databank of Children for not less than three months and confirmation of impossibility of placing this child for custody in the family of the citizens of the Russian Federation continuously residing within the Russian Federation, or for the adoption by relatives of the child irrespective of the citizenship and place of residence of these relatives.

If it is necessary the Court may require some other information. (*Amended on June 25, 1998 # 90-FL*)

After the petition and all the required documents have been filed, the Judge shall find the determination and require from the Bodies of Trusteeship and Guardianship all the above-mentioned documents concerning the child being adopted. The Judge has the right to request any other documents, if he (she) finds it necessary.

Article 263.4. Court Hearing on a petition for adoption

The Court considers cases related to the adoption of children with the obligatory participation of the adoptive parents (parent), a representative of a Body of Trusteeship and Guardianship, and also the Prosecutor.

When it is necessary, the Court may involve in the proceeding, the natural parents (parent) or other legal representatives of the child being adopted, his (her) relatives and other interested persons, and also the child himself (herself) if the child is ten years of age or older.

The Court considers cases related to the adoption of children at the closed hearing. *(Amended on June 25, 1998 # 90-FL)*

Commentary to article 263.4

Part 1 of article 263.4 of the Code of Civil Procedure provides the obligatory personal participation in the adoption hearing of the petitioner, a representative of a Body of Trusteeship and Guardianship, and also the Prosecutor. The failure of the Court to comply with these demands of the law may be the basis for the reversal of the Court decision.

The presence of a petitioner's representative, duly authorized to appear for the petitioner in the Court, does not release the person (persons) who wish to adopt the child from the obligation to be present in the Court. In relation to the cases of this category the representatives are entitled to perform the action without the personal participation of the trustee outside the stage of the Court proceeding, in particular, to collect and to present the required evidence, to give the explanation to the Judge on the merits of the petition while the case is being prepared for hearing, to present the additional evidence after the demand of the Judge, to raise the question about the assistance in requiring written and material evidence, etc.

For the purpose of ensuring the privacy of adoption protected by the law (article 139 of the Family Code of the Russian Federation) the Court, according to part 3 of article 263.4 of the Code of Civil Procedure, considers all cases of this category at the closed hearing. For the same purpose, the persons participating in the proceeding (except for the adoptive parents) shall be notified about the necessity to keep the information about the adoption, which has become known to them secret, and also about the possibility of being criminally responsible for disclosing the secret of adoption against the will of the adoptive parent in cases, specified in article 155 of the Criminal Code of the Russian Federation. This requirement does not cover the adoptive parents, since it is the right of the adoptive parents. This provision protects the rights of the adoptive parents in case the adoptive parents want to keep the fact of adoption private.

Article 263.5. The Court decision on the petition for adoption

The Court, having considered the petition for the adoption of the child substantial, shall issue the Court decision granting or dismissing the adoption fully or in part concerning the request of the adoptive parents (parent) for recording them as the parents (parent) of the child in his (her) birth record, and also the request for the change in the date and place of birth of the child.

If the petition for adoption is granted, mutual rights and obligations of the adoptive parents (parent) and the child being adopted shall be established after the effective date of the Court decision of adoption.

A copy of the Court decision, which has rendered such Court decision, shall be transmitted by the Court to a Body of Civil State Registration corresponding to the place of issuing the Court decision within three days after the effective date of the Court decision for the state registration of the adoption of the child.

Commentary to article 263.5

After the Court hearing, the Judge shall retire to a separate room, which is called "the retiring room" to issue the Court decision.

Nobody is allowed to enter this room, including the Attorney, the Clerk of the Court and other persons, while the Judge is issuing the Court decision. It is prohibited while the Judge is making the judgment. According to the law, the Judge shall make the decision under the conditions eliminating the possibility of receiving someone's advice or recommendations given in any form (orally, in writing, over the telephone, etc.). Even the unintended violation of the privacy of breaking the case (an occasional call and talk over the telephone, an open door) may be the basis for assessing these facts as the violation of the privacy of the retiring room and be the basis for reversing the Court decision.

After the Court decision has been awarded, it shall be declared to all the participants of the proceeding. The Court is obligated within three days to transmit a copy of the Court decision to the Bodies of Civil State Registration. In practice, in order to forward the process of receiving the certificate of adoption and the certificate of birth, the adoptive parents themselves deliver the Court decision to The Bodies of Civil State Registration.

If there are some exceptional circumstances, owing to which the delay in the performance of the adoption Court decision can lead to the impossibility of the performance, the Court, proceeding from clause 3 of article 211 of the Code of Civil Procedure, has the right at the request of the petitioner or on its own initiative to enforce the Court decision into effect immediately, having specified the reasons, according to which it has come to the conclusion about the necessity to apply the said regulation (for example, the emergency hospitalization of the child being adopted is required to give him (her) a Course of treatment and (or) to perform an operation, and the delay threatens the life and health of the child). The reasons may be different and it depends on a particular Court and Judge. For some of the Judges any circumstance is valid (even such as the return tickets, and the necessity to come back to work), for other Judges a valid circumstance can be only the critical condition of the child, when he (she) needs an emergency hospitalization or operation.

SECTION III

Chapter 34

APPEAL AND PROTEST
THE COURT DECISIONS

Article 282. The right to appeal and protest against the Court decision

The Court decisions of all Courts of the Russian Federation, except for the judgments of the Supreme Court of the Russian Federation, may be appealed by the parties and other persons participating in the procedure, to a Superior Court.

The Prosecutor or the Deputy Prosecutor enters the protest against the wrongful or groundless Court decision, irrespective of the fact whether he (she) participated in this case. The assistant Prosecutor and the Prosecution department may enter protests only concerning the cases, in which they participated.

Commentary to article 282

The law provides three independent stages of civil procedure to amend possible errors of Courts made during the proceeding and disposition of the case, and to remove the doubts of the persons participating in the case, in the propriety of judgments and determinations.

The appeal against the judgments and determinations, which have not come into effect, is the fastest and most available way to verify the lawfulness and propriety of the rulings by the Court. The exercise of the right to appeal in this stage depends on the will of the persons participating in the case. The appeal to the Superior Court, with the observance of the procedure and period of time prescribed by the law, involves the obligatory consideration of the case by a Superior Court.

If the applicants disagree with the Court decision they may appeal against the Court decision. This right is provided by the law.

Article 283. The procedure of entering an appeal or protest

The Court decisions, which have not come into effect may be appealed and protested against to the Superior Court:

1. The Court decisions of District Courts - to a Regional Court accordingly;

2. The Court decisions of Regional Courts – to the Supreme Court of the Russian Federation.

Appeals and protests are made through the Court, which has issued the Court decision. Appealing or protesting directly to the Superior Court is not the bar for the consideration of the appeal or protest.

Commentary to article 283

As Regional Courts consider the cases related to the Court decision of adoption for persons continuously living outside of the Russian Federation, the Court decisions of these Courts may be appealed to the Supreme Court of the Russian Federation, through that Court, which has rendered the Court decision.

Article 284. Time frame for Appeal or Protest.

An appeal or protest can be made within ten days after the entry of the final Court decision. An appeal or protest made after the expiration of the specified term is left without consideration and is returned back to the person who has made the petition for appeal or protest.

Commentary to article 284

The law establishes the ten-day term for entering an appeal. The beginning of this term is the date, following the date of the entry of the final Court decision.

If the substantive provision of the Court decision was declared, the term for the appeal (protest) against the Court decision shall be calculated since the date, following the date appointed by the Court for learning the reasoned solution.

The petitions or protests made after the expiration of the term specified by article 284 are left without consideration and are returned to the persons who have made them. The refusal to take a petition for appeal shall involve the determination, in which the Court is obligated to specify the reasons for the refusal. The determination of the refusal to take the petition for appeal (protest) can be appealed to the Superior Court according to clause 2 of article 315.

The ten-day term for making an appeal or protest established by the law cannot be reduced or extended under the decision of the Court. If the Court recognizes the reasons according to which the persons have defaulted to the term as valid it may be reestablished.

A special petition for appeal and a special protest can be made against the Court's determination of the refusal to reestablish the term for the appeal.

Article 284-1. Terms of consideration of a case in the Superior Court

The Regional Court shall consider the case on the appeal or protest within 10 days after the date of receiving the case with the petition for appeal (protest). If it is especially hard, or in other exceptional cases the term can be extended, but not more than ten days.

The Supreme Court of the Russian Federation shall consider a case within one month after the date of receiving the case.

Article 286. The contents of an appeal or protest

An appeal or protest shall contain:

1. The title of the Court, to which the petition for appeal or protest is addressed;

2. The name of a person filing the appeal or protest;

3. The notation of the Court decision, which is being appealed or protested against, and the Court, which has rendered this Court decision;

4. The explanation of what constitutes the errors of the solution, and the request of a person filing the petition for appeal or protest.

5. The list of the written documents attached to the petition for appeal or protest.

The reference of the person filing the appeal, to new evidence, which has not been presented to the Court of primary jurisdiction, is allowed only if he (she) has validated the impossibility of its presentation to the Court of primary jurisdiction.

A petition for appeal shall be signed by the person filing the appeal or by his (her) representative. A protest shall be signed by the Prosecutor.

The Power of Attorney or other document certifying the authorities of the representative shall be filed together with the petition for appeal made by the representative if there is no such authority in the case.

Commentary to article 286

An appeal for review is made to the Court of superior juris-diction in relation to the Court, which has rendered the judg-ment. According to article 282 only persons participating in the case may file the petition for appeal.

The persons filing the petition for appeal shall specify in it their position in the procedure (claimant, defendant, applicant, etc.), the surname, name, patronymic name, and the place of residence.

3. Furthermore, it is necessary to name the title of the pro-cedural document (petition for appeal). After that it is neces-sary to point out, what particular Court decision is being appealed against: when (to indicate the date), what Court and regarding what case.

The contents of an appeal are determined by specific cir-cumstances of the case and the contents of the Court decision. In any case the person appealing to the Court shall specify the reasons, according to which he (she) considers the Court deci-sion rendered improper.

If the Attorney files the appeal, it shall contain clearly stat-ed grounds of the appeal and the plea of the violation of the rules of substance or procedural law.

An appeal depending on specific circumstances of the case may contain the request for the reversal or amendment of the Court decision rendered by the Court of primary jurisdiction.

The list of the written documents, enclosed to the appeal, is set forth only if the person appealing has the intent to present such documents to the Superior Court.

In any event, it is necessary to specify in the petition for appeal, that a copy (copies) of this petition be enclosed.

Part 2 of article 286 sets a new rule, according to which a person filing a petition for appeal may plead new evidence, which has not been presented to the Court of primary jurisdiction, only if he (she) has validated in the petition the impossibility of its presentation to the Court of primary jurisdiction.

The establishment of this rule in the Code is explained by the new contents of the principle of adversary civil procedure.

A petition for appeal shall be signed by the person filing the appeal. A protest shall be signed by the Prosecutor.

If the appeal is made and signed by the representative, it is necessary to enclose in the petition for appeal the Power of Attorney certifying the authorities of the representative to enter the appeal.

The appeals on cases related to the adoption of children are free from the Court Fee.

Article 433. Civil procedural rights of foreign citizens, foreign enterprises and organizations

Foreign citizens have the right to apply to the Courts of the Russian Federation and to enjoy civil procedural rights equally with the citizens of Russia.

THE FEDERAL LAW ABOUT THE STATE DATABANK OF CHILDREN WITHOUT PARENTAL CUSTODY

April, 16, 2001   # 44-FL

Chapter I

GENERAL PROVISIONS

Article 1. The basic concepts used in the present Federal Law

In this Federal Law, the following basic concepts are outlined:

The State Databank of Children Without Parental Custody (further-known-as: State Databank of Children) is the aggregate of the information resources generated at a level of subjects of the Russian Federation (a Regional Databank of Children) and at a Federal level (the Federal Databank of Children), and also the information technologies realizing processes of the tax, processing, accruing, storage, search and granting to the persons wishing to accept children for upbringing into their families the documentary information on children who have been left without parental custody and subject to the system for care in families according to the Legislation of the Russian Federation;

The Regional Databank of Children is a part of the State

Databank of Children, containing the documentary information of children who have been left without parental custody living in the territory of one of the regions of the Russian Federation and not arranged by the Bodies of Trusteeship and Guardianship for care in families in the place of actual presence of these children, and also the documentary information of the persons wishing to accept children for upbringing into their families and have requested the appropriate information from the Regional Operator of the State Databank of Children;

The Federal Databank of Children is the part of a State Databank of Children, including the aggregate of Regional Databanks about Children, and also the documentary information on the persons wishing to accept children for upbringing into their families and have requested the appropriate information from the Federal Operator of the State Databank of Children;

The Federal Operator of The State Databank of Children (further known as the Federal Operator) is the Federal Body of Executive Power defined by the Government of the Russian Federation according to article 122 of the Family Code of the Russian Federation;

The Regional Operator of the State Databank of Children (further know as the Regional Operator) is the Body of Executive Power of the regions of the Russian Federation which in the cases established by article 122 of the Family Code of the Russian Federation, should organize the system of the children who have been left without parental custody, or the care of families this opportunity to be placed with a family.

The Citizens (Persons) wishing to accept children for upbringing into their families are the Russian Citizens continuously residing in a territory of the Russian Federation and wishing to adopt children without parental custody or to accept them under trusteeship (guardianship) or foster family and also the Russian Citizens continuously living outside of the Russian Federation, foreign citizens and persons without citizenship, wishing to adopt children who have been left without parental custody, if there is the basis established by the legislation of the Russian Federation.

Article 2. The Legislation of the State Databank of Children

The Legislation of the State Databank of Children is based on provisions of the Constitution of the Russian Federation, the Family Code of the Russian Federation, Federal Acts in the field of information, information and protections of the information and consists of the present Federal Law and other Legal Acts of the Russian Federation, and also Laws and other Legal Acts of the subjects of the Russian Federation.

Article 3. The purposes of formation and use of a State Databank of Children

The purposes of the formation and use of a State Databank of Children are:

The creation of standards of documentation and information of children who have been left without parental custody;

The rendering of assistance for the children who have been left without parental custody, to be placed into families of Russian Citizens continuously living in the territory of the Russian Federation;

The creation of conditions for realization of the right of the citizens (persons) wishing to accept children for upbringing into their families upon receiving complete and reliable information about children who have been left without parental custody.

Article 4. Obligatory requests to the formation and use of the State Databank of Children

1. Obligatory requests to the formation and use of a State Databank of Children are:

Standardization of the documentary information on children who have been left without parental custody, and the citizens (persons) wishing to accept children for upbringing into their families and the technical program, technical maintenance (including unification of processes of input, processing, storage, recovering, duplication and granting of the indicated information) with the purposes of the creation of the uniform communication environment of Regional Databanks of Children and the Federal Databank of Children;

The use of the information on children who have been left without parental custody, and the citizens (persons) wishing to accept children for upbringing into their families only for the purposes of formation and use of a State Databank of Children;

The completeness and certainty of the documentary information on children who have been left without parental custody, and the citizens (persons) wishing to accept children for upbringing into their families;

The protection of the documentary information against outflow, plunder, loss, fabrication, distortion and the non-authorized access to it.

2. The State Databank of Children is formed as the information resources that are taking place in the joint conducting of the Russian Federation and subjects of the Russian Federation.

3. The State Registration of the Databank of Children is carried out by the Federal Body of Executive Power in the field of communication and information.

4. Information Technologies, which are intended for processing the State Databank of Children, are subject to obligatory certification within the system of certification of the Federal Body of Executive Power in the field of communication and information.

Chapter II

FORMATION OF THE STATE DATABANK OF CHILDREN

Article 5. Obligatory granting of data for the formation of the State Databank of Children

1. For the formation of a Regional Databank of Children, Bodies of Trusteeship and Guardianship that are obligated to give the Regional Operator information of each child who has been left without parental custody and have not arranged to be placed into a family established by article 122 of the Family Code of the Russian Federation.

2. For formation of the Federal Databank of Children, Regional Operators are obligated to provide the Federal Operator with information on children who have been left without parental custody, if in time, established by article 122 of the Family Code of the Russian Federation, they did not manage to organize the device of these children to be placed into families of Russian citizens continuously living in the territory of the Russian Federation.

3. The bodies specified in items 1 and 2 of the present Article, who are obligated to provide information on children who have been left without parental custody for formation of the State Databank of Children, do not lose the rights of use of this Databank.

Granting information on children who have been left without parental custody to Regional or Federal Operators does not release The Bodies of the Trusteeship and Guardianship, Bodies of Executive Power of subjects of the Russian Federation from the obligation to place these children into families of Russian citizens continuously living in the territory of the Russian Federation.

4. A persons wishing to accept a child for upbringing into his/her family must provide information on himself/herself to the Regional or the Federal Operator.

Article 6. The documentary information on children who have been left without parental custody

1. The documentary information on children, who have been left without parental custody, in the Questionnaire Form of the Child Without Parental Custody (further known as the

Questionnaire Form of the Child), is created according to article 3 of the present Federal Law.

2. The Questionnaire Form of the Child includes the following information:

1) Surname, name, patronymic name, sex, date of birth and birth- place, citizenship, residence or the location of the child who has been left without parental custody;

2) Physical information of the child who has been left without parental custody (height, weight, color of eyes, hair and other attributes);

3) State of health of the child who has been left without parental custody, his/her physical and intellectual development;

4) Features of character of the child who has been left without parental custody (social, closed and other features);

5) Ethnic origin of the child who has been left without parental custody;

6) The reasons of absence of parental custody over the child;

7) Full names, dates of birth, citizenship, religion and culture, state of health (if this information is proven with documentary confirmation) a residence and (or) a place of stay of parent/parents of the child who has been left without parental custody;

8) Full name(s) sex, date(s) of birth, state of health, a residence and (or) the location of minor sibling(s) of the child who has been left without parental custody (if this information is proofed with documentary confirmation);

9) Surnames, names, patronymic names, dates of birth, a residence and (or) a place of stay of other legal age relatives of the child who has been left without parental custody, that are known to the Bodies of Trusteeship and Guardianship, essential elements of the documents confirming refusal of the specified relatives to accept this child for care into their families;

10) Possible forms of placing the child who has been left without parental custody, into a family;

11) The information on the steps taken by the Bodies of Trusteeship and Guardianship, the Regional and the Federal Operator accordingly on the placing and rendering of assistance in the placing of the child who has been left without parental custody, into the family of Russian citizens continuously living in the territory of the Russian Federation;

12) The termination of the account of information on the child who has been left without parental custody, in the Federal Databank of Children. (with the indication of the reasons).

The photo of the child, who has stayed without parental custody, should be applied to the Questionnaire Form of the Child.

Article 7. The documentary information on the citizens (persons) wishing to accept children for upbringing into their families

1. The documentary information on a person wishing to accept a child for upbringing into his/her family (the Questionnaire Form of the Person Wishing to Accept the Child (further referenced as the Questionnaire Form of the Person), is created for the purpose to register information on that person in the State Databank of Children and the providing of access of that person to documentary information contained in the Regional Databank and the Federal Databank of Children of the documentary information on children who have been left without parental custody.

2. Documenting of the information on the citizens (persons) wishing to accept children for upbringing into their families is carried out on the written application on the basis established by the Law to be adoptive parents, trustees or foster parents.

Before documenting the information on the person wishing to accept a child for upbringing into his/her family, the Regional or the Federal Operator is obligated to acquaint this person with the list of the documentary information, the basis and the purpose of documenting this information and the order of its use.

3. The Questionnaire Form of the Person includes the following information:

1) The surname, name, patronymic name, sex, birth date and birth place, citizenship, marital status, residence and (or) a place of stay, contact phone number and essential

elements of the identification document of the person wishing to accept the child for upbringing into his/her family;

2) Essential elements of the Homestudy on a residence of the person wishing to accept the child for upbringing into his/her family about his/her ability to be adoptive parents, the trustee or the foster parent. Essential elements of Homestudy that indicated the conditions of life and an ability of the Russian citizens continuously living outside of the Russian Federation, foreign citizens, or the person without the citizenship to be adoptive parents for children who are Russian Citizens. It must be appropriate to the legislation on adoption of the State in which the specified citizen or the person has a permanent residence;

3) The description of the child of the persons wishing to accept children for upbringing into their families;

4) The information on the referrals given out to this person wishing to accept the child for upbringing into his/her family for visiting the chosen child, that has stayed without parental custody. Information must indicate date of issue of the referral and full name of child;

5) The information on the decision of this person on acceptance of the child who has been left without parental custody, on placing him/her into the family or about refusal of acceptance of that decision with the indication of the reasons of refusal;

6) The information on the termination of the account of information in the State Databank on the citizens (persons) wishing to accept a child for upbringing into their family (with the indication of the reasons);

Article 8. The confidential information on children who have been left without parental custody, and the citizens (persons) wishing to accept children for upbringing into their families

1. The Questionnaire Form of the Child and the Questionnaire Form of the Person of Concern, according to the legislation of the Russian Federation, is considered as confidential information. The order of access to the confidential information on children who have been left without parental custody, and the citizens (persons) wishing to accept children for upbringing into their families is defined by article 11 of the present Federal Law.

2. The confidential information on children who have been left without parental custody can be used by Regional and the Federal Operators for creation of the derivative information on children who have been left without parental custody, and distribution of the specified information by means of publication in mass media or a different way with a view of informing the population of the Russian Federation on children staying without parental custody and subject to the device on care in families. Use of the derivative information on children that has stayed without parental custody, for commercial purpose is not permissible.

At the creation and distribution of the specified information, the opportunity of identification of the person of the child who has been left without parental custody, his (her) parents and his (her) other relatives, should be excluded.

The derivative information on children who have been left without parental custody is the information such as sex, age and physical attributes, except for certain specific physical attributes, state of health, physical and intellectual development, features of character of such children, the reasons of absence of parental custody, state of health of their parents, presence of the child's siblings, their age and state of health, presence of legal age relatives and the information on their refusal to accept these children into their families, and also possible forms of the placing these children into families and photos of the children.

Article 9. The termination of the account of information on children who have been left without parental custody and the citizens (persons) wishing to accept children for upbringing into their families in the State Databank of Children

1. The grounds of the termination of the account of the information on the child who has been left without parental custody, in the State Databank of Children are:

The placing of the child who has been left without the parental custody, into the family;

Returning of a child who has been left without parental custody, to his/her parents or the parent;

Achievement by the child, who has stayed without parental custody, of full;

Death of a child who has been left without parental custody.

2. The grounds of the termination of the account of the information on the citizens (persons) wishing to accept a child for upbringing into their family in the State Databank about children is;

Acceptance by the person of the child for placing into his/her family;

The written petition of the person wishing to accept a child for upbringing into his/her family of the termination of the account of information on him/her in the State Databank of Children;

Change of circumstances, which gave the person a disability to accept the child into the family;

Death of the person wishing to accept a child for upbringing into his/her family.

Chapter III

USE OF THE STATE DATABANK OF CHILDREN

Article 10. The order of use of the State Databank of Children

1. Access to the State Databank of Children is provided by the Regional Operators and the Federal Operator by means of publication in mass media or other distributions of data on the activity (a location, the order and a mode of operation, the list of given services and other information).

2. The citizens (persons) wishing to accept children for upbringing into their family have the right to apply for information about children who have been left without parental custody, to any Regional Operator or Federal Operator of their choice.

3. Obligatory conditions of reception of the documentary information on children who have been left without parental custody, from a Regional Databank of Children or a Federal Databank of Children are: the written applications of the person wishing to accept the child for upbringing into his/her family should be submitted with the request to acquaint him/her with the appropriate information on all eligible children according to the adopters description and observance by him/her of the order for access to the confidential information established by article 11 of the present Federal law.

4. The Regional Operator or Federal Operator, no later than ten days from the date of reception of the written application, is obligated to consider it in essence and to provide to the person wishing to accept a child for upbringing into his/her family required by him/her documentary information or to give a motivated refusal in writing in its granting. That refusal must contain the grounds on which the required documentary information cannot be provided, date of decision making about that refusal, and also the order of the appeal of that decision.

5. Regional or the Federal Operators are obligated to provide to the citizens (persons) wishing to accept children for upbringing into their families, under their requests the information on the legal acts, regulating conditions and the order of the device of children who have been left without parental custody, into families, and also help, advisory and other materials which can assist people for the decision of questions on reception of children who have been left without parental custody, into the families.

6. Bodies of Trusteeship and Guardianship, the Regional and Federal Operator carry this out using the Regional Data-

banks of Children and a Federal Databank of Children by means of an exchange of official information.

During the exchange of information, the Regional and the Federal Operators are obligated to provide protection of the confidential information on children who have been left without parental custody, and the citizens (persons) wishing to accept children for upbringing into their families in order to prevent the non-authorized access to it or its casual or non-authorized change, destruction or loss.

Each case of an exchange of the specified confidential information is subject to obligatory registration.

7. Use of the State Databank of Children is available free-of-charge.

Article 11. The order of access to the confidential information on children who have been left without parental custody, and citizens (persons) wishing to accept children for upbringing into their families

1. Access of the citizens (persons) wishing to accept children for upbringing into their families to the confidential information on children who have been left without parental custody is carried out under the condition of documenting the information on the people in the order established by article 7 of the present Federal Law.

2. The Russian citizens continuously living outside of the Russian Federation, foreign citizens and stateless persons, wishing to adopt the child without parental custody and eligible for placing the child into the referenced persons family,

have the right to access the confidential information only under the conditions established by the Family Code of the Russian Federation and the condition that the Questionnaire of the Child consists of the information about the steps taken by the Bodies of Trusteeship and Guardianship, Regional and Federal Operators to place the child into a Russian family residing continuously within the Russian Federation.

3. The right of access to the confidential information on the citizens (persons) wishing to accept children for upbringing into their families and the right of entering the necessary changes and additions of the persons that have access only to the confidential information which is documented.

4. The Regional Operators and the Federal Operator are obligated to provide the confidential information on children who have been left without parental custody and the citizens (persons) wishing to accept children for upbringing into their families to Court, Bodies of Office of the Public Prosecutor, Bodies of Inquiry or Investigation or to the Representative under Human Rights in the Russian Federation on their inquiries.

Article 12. The order of providing to people the confidential information on children who have been left without parental custody

1. The confidential information on children, who have been left without parental custody, is given in writing personally to the people about whom there is appropriate documented information in the Federal Databank of Children in the time frame established by article 10 of the present Federal Law.

The specified confidential information is given to the people under their request about all children who have been staying without parental custody, the documentary information which is contained in the Regional Databank of Children or The Federal Databank of Children and corresponds to the information on the child, which the person would wish to accept into their family.

In the case that more than one person has specified the identical information on the same children, a priority in obtaining the appropriate confidential information on the children who have been left without parental custody goes to the person who has the earlier of his/her account of information in the State Databank of Children.

2. At the time when a person wishing to accept a child for upbringing into their family makes a choice of the child who has been left without parental custody, the Federal or Regional Operator of the Databank of Children provides the referral to visit this child with the notice of the Body of Trusteeship and Guardianship in a place of residence of the child who has been left without parental custody. At the same time when the referral was issued, a note should be made in the Questionnaire of the Child and the Questionnaire of the Person regarding this action.

3. In case the appropriate information required by the person is absent in the Regional Databank of Children or the Federal Databank of Children, the written application of this person and the search of the child that the person would wish to accept into their family must proceed, or the account of information on this person in the State Databank of Children terminates.

A notice in writing must be sent by the Regional/Federal Operator to the person wishing to accept the child for upbringing into his/her family about the results of the search of the specified child in each case of the receipt of new information on children who have been left without parental custody, but not less often than once a month.

Article 13. Protection of the rights of people on receiving of the information

Unreasonable refusal to access to the State Databank of Children, granting unreliable information about children who have been left without parental custody, concealment of that information and other wrongful actions violating the rights of people on receiving the specified information or creating obstacles to the realization of such rights, can be appealed against the refusal in Court in the order established by the Civil Procedure Legislation.

Article 14. The liability for violation of the present Federal Law

Persons guilty of violation of the present Federal Law bear the responsibility according to the legislation of the Russian Federation.

Article 15. The order of conducting the State Databank of Children and the procedure of the control of its formation and use

The order of conducting the State Databank of Children and

the procedure of the control of its formation and use are defined by the Government of the Russian Federation.

Chapter IV

FINAL PROVISIONS

Article 16. Coming into force of the present Federal Law

1. The present Federal Law goes into effect six months from the date of its official publication.

2. Before the present Federal Law goes into effect, the centralized account of children who have been left without parental custody is carried out in the order established by Government of the Russian Federation.

Article 17. About reduction of legal acts conformity with the present Federal Law

Government of the Russian Federation within six months from the date of enactment of the present Federal Law should:

Bring all Legal Acts into accord with the present Federal Law;

Issue the Legal Acts providing realization of the present Federal Law.

The President of
Russian Federation

V. PUTIN

Moscow, The Kremlin
April 16, 2001
44-FL

THE RULES
OF KEEPING THE STATE DATABANK
OF CHILDREN WITHOUT PARENTAL
CUSTODY AND ITS FORMATION AND
USE CONTROL
(Excerpts)

Approved by the Governmental Regulation of the Russian Federation of
April 4, 2002 #217

I. The registration of children who have been left without parental custody

1. The State Databank of Children without parental custody (hereinafter cited as the State Databank of Children) is the complex of information resources formed at the level of the subjects of the Russian Federation, that is the Regional Databank of Children, and at the Federal level, that is the Federal Databank of Children, and also of information technologies providing the citizens (persons) wishing to accept children for upbringing into their families with the documentary information about the children who have been left without parental custody and are subject to placement with adoptive families.

2. The officials of preschool institutions, comprehensive schools, prophylactic and other institutions, and citizens who have the information about the children who have been left without parental custody shall inform about this the Bodies of Trusteeship and Guardianship corresponding to the place of physical presence of the children.

The heads of educational, prophylactic and social service institutions and other similar establishments where the children left without parental custody are held shall inform about this the Body of Trusteeship and Guardianship corresponding to the institution location within 7 days following the date of receiving the information that the child may be placed for care with a family.

3. The Body of Trusteeship and Guardianship shall complete the report of the child's living conditions within 3 days after the date of receiving the information about a child who has been left without parental custody, and when the fact is found that the parental custody is missing, shall register the information about the child in the book of initial registration of children who have been left without parental custody, and shall also provide temporary placement of the child up to the decision of placing the child with a family or in the institution for orphan children and the children who have been left without parental custody.

The initial registration of children who have been left without parental custody and the execution of documents for placing the children for upbringing into the family are realized by the Body of Trusteeship and Guardianship corresponding to the place of physical presence of the child.

4. If the child who has been left without parental custody, in regard to whom there had arisen the grounds established under the law to place him (her) for upbringing into a family, has not been placed in a family according to the place of his (her) actual presence the Body of Trusteeship and Guardianship completes his (her) Questionnaire of the Child Left Without Parental Custody (hereinafter cited as the Questionnaire of the Child) which is transmitted within 7 days to the appropriate

Regional Operator of the State Databank of Children (here-inafter cited as the Regional Operator) for entering the information about the child in the Regional Databank of Children.

The Questionnaire of the Child is signed by the worker of the Body of Trusteeship and Guardianship.

The photograph is attached to the Questionnaire of the Child.

The copy of the Questionnaire of the Child is kept at the Body of Trusteeship and Guardianship and in the child's personal file at the institution where the child is held.

5. The Regional Operator forms the Regional Databank of children on the grounds of the information about the children left without parental custody which has been transmitted from the Bodies of Trusteeship and Guardianship and realizes the registration of the children and organizes their placement for upbringing in the families of citizens of the Russian Federation continuously residing within the Russian Federation.

The entry date of the information about the child left without parental custody in the Regional Databank of Children shall be the date when the Regional Operator receives the Questionnaire of the Child executed under the established procedure.

If the child who has been left without parental custody has not been, within the month following the entry date of the information about him (her), in the Regional Databank of Children placed for care with a family, the Regional Operator within 3 days transmits the copy of the Questionnaire of the Child and the photo of the child to the Federal Operator of the

State Databank of Children (hereinafter known as the Federal Operator).

6. The Federal Operator forms the Federal Databank of Children on the ground of the information about the children left without parental custody which has been transmitted from the Regional Databanks of Children and realizes the registration of the children and promotes their placement for care in the families of citizens of the Russian Federation continuously residing within the Russian Federation.

The entry date of the information about a child who has been left without parental custody in the Federal Databank of Children shall be the date when the Federal Operator receives the copy of the Questionnaire of the Child.

7. If the information of the Questionnaire of the Child has been changed, the Body of Trusteeship and Guardianship and the Regional Operator must within 3 days inform the Regional Operator and Federal Operator respectively.

The Body of Trusteeship and Guardianship and the Regional Operator direct to the Regional and Federal Databank of Children respectively the photographs of children who have been left without parental custody:

once a year when the child is under three years of age;

once in three years when the child is from three to eighteen years of age.

8. If the child who has been left without parental custody has been transferred from the institution of one subject of the Russian Federation to the institution of another subject of the

Russian Federation, the Body of Trusteeship and Guardianship within 3 days informs about this the Regional Operator corresponding to the location of the institution from which the child has been transferred. The Regional Operator within 3 days transmits the child from to the Regional Databank of Children of the subject of the Russian Federation to the institution of which the child left without parental custody has been transferred, and informs the Federal Operator.

9. The information about the steps taken by the Body of Trusteeship and Guardianship and by the Regional and Federal Operator to arrange and promote the placement of children who have been left without parental custody with the families of citizens of the Russian Federation continuously residing within the Russian Federation is entered in the Questionnaire of the Child and is directed to the Regional and Federal Databank of Children respectively within 3 days following the day on which:

a) the citizen (person) wishing to accept the child for upbringing into his/her family learns the information about children who have been left without parental custody;

b) the citizen (person) wishing to accept the child for upbringing into his/her family is granted a referral to visit the child who has been left without parental custody;

c) the citizen wishing to take the child for care into the family files the statement of the effect of visiting a child who has been left without parental custody;

d) the information about the children who have been left without parental custody which is not confidential is published in mass media or disseminated in some other way.

II. The functions of the Regional Operator and the Federal Operator on keeping the State Databank of Children

10. The Regional Operator and Federal Operator:

a) register the children who have been left without parental custody;

b) register the information about the petitioners wishing to accept the child for upbringing into their family;

c) inform the citizens (persons) who wish to accept the child for upbringing into their family about the procedure of providing the information about the child who has left without parental custody which is available in the State Databank of Children, and about the list of documentary information about the citizen (person), the grounds and purposes of documenting this information and its use procedure;

d) consider the documents of citizens (persons) who wish to accept the child for upbringing into their family;

e) document the information about the citizens (persons) who wish to accept the child for upbringing into their family;

f) provide the information about the children who have been left without parental custody for the citizens (persons) wishing to accept the child for upbringing into their family whose information has been entered in the State Databank of Children;

g) grant to the citizens (persons) wishing to accept the child for upbringing into their family a referral to visit the child left who has been without parental custody selected by them;

h) organize the work on apprising the population of the Russian Federation of the children who have been left without parental custody and are subject to placement for upbringing into families;

i) provide the citizens (persons) wishing to accept the child for upbringing into their family with the information about the appropriate statutory legal acts and reference materials and counsel them of the issues of placing the children who have been left without parental custody for care with families.

IV. The registration of information about the citizens of the Russian Federation continuously residing outside the Russian Federation, foreign citizens and stateless persons wishing to adopt the children who have been left without parental custody

19. Documenting of the information about a citizen of the Russian Federation continuously residing outside the Russian Federation, a foreign citizen or a stateless person wishing to adopt the child and for this purpose to learn the information about the children who have been left without parental custody which is available in the State Databank of Children is executed by the appropriate operator.

A citizen of the Russian Federation continuously residing outside the Russian Federation, a foreign citizen or a stateless person has the right after the expiration of three months following the date of entering the information about the child who has been left without parental custody in the State Databank of Children to receive the information only about the child in regard to whom the grounds for adoption established by the law have arisen.

20. A citizen of the Russian Federation continuously residing outside the Russian Federation, a foreign citizen or a stateless person produce to the appropriate operator the identifying document recognized by the Russian Federation in this capacity and forward:

a) the application containing the desire of the petitioner to adopt the child and the request to provide him (her) with the information available in the State Databank of Children about the children meeting his (her) criteria;

b) the completed Questionnaire of the Person;

c) the obligation to register the adopted child under the established procedure at the appropriate Consular Office of the Russian Federation;

d) the obligation to provide the opportunity for completing post-placement supervisory reports for adopted children;

e) the copy of the identification document of the Russian Federation citizen continuously residing outside the Russian Federation, or of a foreign citizen or a stateless person recognized by the Russian Federation in this capacity;

f) the Homestudy completed by the specially authorized organization in the State of citizenship (in the State of permanent residence for a citizen of the Russian Federation continuously residing outside the Russian Federation or for a stateless person) of the living conditions and the possibility to be an adoptive parent. The family photo materials are attached to the Homestudy;

g) the obligation of a specially authorized organization in the State of residence of the citizen of the Russian Federation continuously residing outside the Russian Federation, or of a foreign citizen, or a stateless person to provide the supervision of the adopted child's living conditions and upbringing and to complete post-placement supervisory reports for the adopted child with the family of the adoptive parent;

h) the obligation of a specially authorized organization in the State of residence of the citizen of the Russian Federation continuously residing outside the Russian Federation, or a foreign citizen, to check the registration of the adopted child at the consular office of the Russian Federation;

i) the copy of the license (or of another document) of a foreign agency, verifying the qualification and authority to complete the documents specified in sub-clauses "f" – "h" of this clause.

21. In case of going to another country at the moment of the adoption proceeding for a period of more than one year (to work or by other reasons) a citizen of the Russian Federation continuously residing outside the Russian Federation, a foreign citizen or a stateless person besides the documents specified in sub-clauses a) – f) of clause 20 of these Rules enters the following documents:

a) the conclusion of the possibility to be an adoptive parent and the obligation to provide the supervision of the adopted child's living conditions and care and the child's registration at the Consular Office of the Russian Federation on return to the state of permanent residence issued by a specially authorized organization;

b) the conclusion of the child's living conditions and the obligation to provide the supervision of the living conditions and care of the adopted child and the child's registration at the Consular Office of the Russian Federation on arrival in the State on the territory of which the citizen resides at the moment of the adoption proceeding issued by a specially authorized organization.

22. A citizen of the Russian Federation continuously residing outside the Russian Federation, or a foreign citizen continuously residing within the state of which he (she) is not a citizen puts in the documents specified in sub-clauses "f" - "i" of clause 20 of these Rules, issued by a specially authorized organization in the state of his (her) permanent residence.

23. All documents being submitted according to clauses 20 and 21 of these Rules shall be legalized under the established procedure, except as otherwise provided, under the Legislation of the Russian Federation or under the International Treaty of the Russian Federation, and shall be translated into the Russian language, and the signature of the translator shall be certified at the Consular Office or the Diplomatic Agency of the Russian Federation in the state of residence of the citizen of the Russian Federation continuously residing outside the Russian Federation, a foreign citizen or a stateless person, or by a notary within the Russian Federation.

The documents specified in sub-clauses "a" – "d" of clause 20 are admitted to consideration within one year following the date of their execution and the documents specified in sub-clauses "f" - "i" of this clause are admitted to consideration within one year following the date of their issue.

If the legislation of a foreign state provides another term of validity of the documents specified in sub-clauses "f" - "i" they may be considered within the term established by the legislation of this state.

24. The appropriate operator within 10 days after the date of receipt of the application and all the necessary documents considers them on the merits and provides a citizen of the Russian Federation continuously residing outside the Russian Federation, a foreign citizen or a stateless person with the form and the photo of the child left without parental custody and meeting his (her) desire to be learned or gives him (her) the documents back specifying in writing the reasons of denial to grant the requested information about a child who has been left without parental custody.

25. The referral to visit the selected child is granted to a citizen of the Russian Federation continuously residing outside the Russian Federation, a foreign citizen or a stateless person according to the following procedure:

When a citizen has selected a child who has been left without parental custody, the appropriate operator grants him (her) the referral to visit this child and within 3 days informs the Body of Trusteeship and Guardianship or the Regional Operator corresponding to the place of physical presence of the specified child about this action.

The referral is granted for the visit to only one child and is valid within 10 days following the date of its issue. This time frame may be extended by the appropriate operator should there be extenuating circumstances preventing the person to visit the child during this time (an illness, business trip, etc.).

If the referral to visit a child who has been left without parental custody is granted to one citizen (person) the information about this child cannot be disclosed at the same time to another citizen.

The citizen (person) is obligated within the term established for visiting a child who has been left without parental custody to inform in writing the appropriate operator about the results of the visit to the child and the decision made.

If the citizen (person) refuses to take the offered child for upbringing into his (her) family, he (she) is granted the referral to visit another child selected by him (her).

26. If, in the Regional or Federal Databank of Children, there is no information about a child who has been left without parental custody meeting the specific criteria of the applicant, the search of the child who has been left without parental custody may be continued as follows:

The citizen (person) has the right to file the petition for the search of such child;

The appropriate operator not less than once a month notifies the citizen (person) in writing about the incoming (or no change of) new Questionnaire of the Child containing the information that meets the desires of the citizen;

The citizen (person) may obtain the new Questionnaire of the Child within 15 days after receiving such notification;

The specified term may be extended if the citizen (person), within 15 days after receiving the notification, informs the appropriate operator about the grounds preventing him (her) from learning about the new Questionnaire of the Child (an illness, a business trip, etc.);

If the citizen (person) has received notification twice of the search results of the child left without parental custody and has not come to learn about the new Questionnaire of the Child, the search of the child who has been left without parental custody for this citizen is suspended and may be proceeded on the ground of the written petition of the citizen.

27. If a citizen of the Russian Federation continuously residing outside the Russian Federation, a foreign citizen or a stateless person whose information is not present in the State Databank of Children became acquainted with a child who has been left without parental custody and has expressed the desire to adopt him (her), he (she) has, under the established procedure, to provide the information about himself (herself) for the appropriate Regional Databank of Children.

28. To solve the adoption case of a child who has been left without parental custody the Regional Operator within 10 days after receiving the petition of a citizen of the Russian Federation continuously residing outside the Russian Federation, of a foreign citizen, or a stateless person for the adoption of the selected child directs the letter of request to the Federal Operator asking to verify the presence of the information about the specific child in the State Databank of Children.

In the letter of request the Regional Operator indicates the surname, name, patronymic name and the date of birth of the child left without parental custody, the surname, name, the country of residence and the address of the citizen adopting the child, the name and address of the specially authorized organization which has completed the appropriate Homestudy for him (her) and has taken the responsibility to provide the supervision of the adopted child's living conditions and upbringing; and the name and address of the foreign agency representing the interests of this citizen within the Russian Federation. The specified information is written in Russian and in the language of the country where the adoptive parent resides.

The Federal Operator, within 10 days following the date of receiving this letter of inquiry, confirms in writing the presence of the information about a child who has been left without parental custody in the State Databank of Children and the impossibility to place him (her) within the established time under the Legislation of the Russian Federation term for upbringing in the family of citizens of the Russian Federation continuously residing within the Russian Federation.

29. A citizen of the Russian Federation continuously residing outside the Russian Federation, a foreign citizen or a stateless person shall inform the appropriate operator in writing within 10 days:

a) about filing the petition for adoption with the Court;

b) about the adoption decision of the Court;

c) about the decision to terminate the research of the child and to discontinue the registration of information about him (her) in the State Databank of Children.

V. The control over the formation and use of the State Databank of Children

30. The Regional and Federal Operators control the proper way of filling out the Questionnaire of the Person.

The appropriate operator returns the incorrectly completed Questionnaire of the Person back to the citizen (person) on the day of the form submission.

31. The Regional Operator controls the observation by the Bodies of Trusteeship and Guardianship and the institutions where the children left without parental custody are kept of the procedure of disclosing the information about children used for the formation of the Regional Databank of Children.

The incorrectly completed form is given by the Regional Operator back to the Body of Trusteeship and Guardianship within 3 days after the date of its reception in order to fully complete it under the established procedure.

The appropriate Body of Trusteeship and Guardianship bears the responsibility for the violation of the terms of transmitting the information about the children who have been left without parental custody to the Regional Databank of Children.

32. The Regional Operator checks annually:

a) the correspondence of the number of children who have been left without parental custody and registered in the Regional Databank of Children with the number of children who have been left without parental custody and held in educational, prophylactic and social service institutions and other similar institutions where the children who have been left without parental custody are held;

b) the observance by the Bodies of Trusteeship and Guardianship:

of the terms of transmission to the Regional Databank of Children of the information about the children who have been left without parental custody and about the discontinuance of the registration of data about the children left without parental custody;

of the procedure of transmitting the information about the change of personal data of the child who has been left without parental custody contained in the Questionnaire of the Child.

33. The Regional Operator regularly directs (not less than once in three months) the information about the results of inspection by the heads of the Bodies of Trusteeship and Guardianship to take the appropriate measures.

34. The Federal Operator controls the observation by the Regional Operator of the procedure of transmitting the information about the children who have been left without parental custody to the Federal Databank of Children.

In case of violation of necessary requirements related to the information about the children who have been left without parental custody, which is transmitted from the Regional to the Federal Databank of Children the Federal Operator within 7 days after the date of receiving the specified information, informs the appropriate Regional Operator about the impossibility to enter this information in the Federal Databank of Children.

The appropriate Regional Operator bears the responsibility for the violation of the terms of transmitting the information about children who have been left without parental custody from the Regional to the Federal Databank of Children.

The Federal Operator systematizes the data about the revealed violation and regularly directs (not less than once in 6 months) the appropriate information to the heads of executive authorities of the subjects of the Russian Federation.

THE RULES OF PLACING CHILDREN FOR ADOPTION AND THE CONTROL OF THEIR LIVING CONDITIONS AND UPBRINGING IN THE FAMILIES OF THE ADOPTIVE PARENTS WITHIN THE RUSSIAN FEDERATION
(Excerpts)

Established by the Government Regulation
of the Russian Federation of March 29, 2000 # 275

I. General Provisions

1. These Rules determine the procedure:

of placing the children who are the citizens of the Russian Federation for adoption by the citizens of the Russian Federation continuously residing within the Russian Federation;

of post-placement supervision of children's living conditions and upbringing in the families of the adoptive parents within the Russian Federation;

of placing the children who are the citizens of the Russian Federation for adoption by the citizens of the Russian Federation continuously residing outside the Russian Federation or with foreign citizens or stateless persons.

2. Adoption is allowed in respect to children under age whose only parent or both parents

have died;

are unknown, declared by the Court as missing or deceased;

have been recognized by the Court as incapable;

have their parental rights removed by the Court;

have executed their consent to adoption according to the established legal procedure;

have not been living together with the child for more than 6 months and have been evading the care and maintenance of the child on the grounds recognized by the Court as unreasonable (except for the cases when the children who are citizens of the Russian Federation are adopted by foreign citizens or stateless persons);

The adoption of a child who has been abandoned, whose parents are unknown, may be granted according to the established procedure provided by the legislation of the Russian Federation when there is an applicable formal note taken by the Bodies of the Interior;

The adoption of the child abandoned in a maternity hospital or other therapeutic and preventive institution may be granted according to the established procedure provided by the legislation of the Russian Federation when there is an applicable formal note taken by the administration of the institution where the child has been abandoned.

3. Any person of either sex who is eighteen years of age or older may be an adoptive parent, except for:

1) persons recognized by Court as incapable or partially capable;

2) marital partners, if one of them is recognized by Court as incapable or partially capable;

3) persons having their parental rights removed by the Court;

4) persons disqualified by the Court from their responsibilities of guardian (the trustee) for inadequate execution of the responsibilities assigned to them by the law;

5) former adoptive parents, if a previous adoption was annulled by the Court through their fault;

6) persons, who cannot realize their parental rights due to their state of health.

7) persons, who at the moment of granting the adoption have no income providing for the adopted child the cost of living, determined in the subject of the Russian Federation where the adoptive parents (parent) live;

8) persons who do not have a permanent place of residence, and also the living quarters meeting the established sanitary and technical requirements;

9) persons having, at the moment of granting the adoption, a previous conviction for an intentional crime against the life or health of human beings.

10) Persons who are not married to each other cannot jointly adopt the same child.

4. The unauthorized third party activities for the purpose of adoption, i.e. any activities of other persons to the effect of selecting and placing children for adoption on behalf of and in the interests of the persons who wish to adopt the child are not allowed as well as the disclosure of information about the child, photo and video filming and conducting the additional medical examination of the adopted child.

11. Prospective adoptive parents have the right:

to receive the detailed information about the child and the information about the existence of his or her relatives;

to apply to a medical institution for conducting an independent medical examination of the child being adopted with the involvement of the representative of the institution at which the child is held according to the procedure established by the Federal Operator of Databank of Children of the Russian Federation and the Ministry of Health of the Russian Federation.

12. Prospective adoptive parents shall personally:

meet the child and make contact;

learn the documents of the child being adopted;

confirm in writing that they have learned the medical report about the child's state of health.

14. The grounds for the adoption procedure in regard to a particular child shall be the Court application of the prospective adoptive parents for granting the decree of adoption that shall be filed with the Court according to the place of residence (presence) of the child under the legislation of civil procedure.

15. When the child being adopted is 10 years of age or older his (her) consent to adoption is required. The consent to adoption shall be found out by the Bodies of Trusteeship and Guardianship and recorded in a separate document or in the report on the propriety of the adoption and its conformity to the interests of the child being adopted.

16. The child's parents may execute their consent to the adoption of the child by a certain person or without specifying a particular person. The consent of the parents to the child's adoption may be given only after the child's birth.

17. The decision of adoption shall be granted by the Court under the legislation of civil procedure.

18. The Body of Trusteeship and Guardianship corresponding to the place of residence (presence) of the child being adopted shall submit to the Court the report on the propriety of the adoption and its conformity with the interests of the child

being adopted including the information about the personal meeting of the adoptive parents (parent) with the child being adopted.

19. The rights and obligations of the adoptive parents and the adopted child shall arise from the effective date of the Court decree on the child's adoption (hereinafter cited the Court decision).

20. The adoptive parents shall personally take the child at his (her) place of residence (presence) on producing the Passport or other document identifying the adoptive parent and the Court decision.

IV. The adoption of children who are citizens of the Russian Federation by the citizens of the Russian Federation continuously residing outside the Russian Federation or by foreign citizens or stateless persons.

24. The adoption of children who are citizens of the Russian Federation by foreign citizens or stateless persons is allowed only in cases when it is evidently not possible to place the children for upbringing into the families of citizens of the Russian Federation continuously residing within the Russian Federation or for adoption with the relatives of the children irrespective of their citizenship and place of residence.

Children may be placed for adoption with the citizens of the Russian Federation continuously residing outside the Russian Federation, or with foreign citizens or stateless persons who are not the relatives of the children after the expiration of 3 months following the date on which the information about these children was registered according to the established procedure at the State Databank of Children without Parental Custody.

25. The Adoption organization specially authorized by a foreign State (hereinafter called a Foreign organization) may represent the interests of citizens of the Russian Federation continuously residing outside the Russian Federation, or of foreign citizens or stateless persons (hereinafter named as prospective adoptive parents) for the purpose of selecting and placing the children for adoption and may also carry out other non-commercial activities related to the protection of their rights within the Russian Federation through their branches established in the Russian Federation according to the legal procedure.

29. The prospective adoptive parents or the adoptive parents shall have the rights and duties specified in clauses 11, 12, and 20 of these Rules.

30. The decree of adoption shall be granted by the Court corresponding to the place of residence (presence) of the child being adopted on the grounds of the petition of the prospective adoptive parents according to the procedure established by the legislation of civil procedure.

31. The Body of Trusteeship and Guardianship corresponding to the place of residence (presence) of the child being adopted shall submit to the Court the conclusion on the propriety of the adoption and its conformity with the interests of the child being adopted including the information about the personal meeting of the adoptive parents (parent) with the child being adopted.

32. The rights and obligations of the adoptive parents and the adopted child shall arise from the effective date of the Court decree.

THE RULES OF THE REGISTRATION OF CHILDREN WHO ARE CITIZENS OF THE RUSSIAN FEDERATION ADOPTED BY FOREIGN CITIZENS OR STATELESS PERSONS AT CONSULAR OFFICES OF THE RUSSIAN FEDERATION

Established by the Regulation of the Russian Federation
of March 29, 2000 # 275

1. These rules determine the registration procedure of children who are citizens of the Russian Federation and are adopted by foreign citizens or stateless persons at a Consular Office of the Russian Federation located within the consular district of the country of residence of the adoptive parents or at a diplomatic agency of the Russian Federation if the specified office is absent. The registration of children at the consular office shall be executed within 3 months following the date of their entry into the country of residence of the adoptive parents.

2. To register the adopted child the adoptive parents shall produce the following documents at a consular office:

1) the petition for the adopted child's registration and two photographs of the child;

2) the certificate of adoption;

3) the identification documents of the adoptive parents and the child (passports).

3. The information about the child shall be entered into the registration card the form of which is approved by the Ministry of Foreign Affairs of the Russian Federation.

4. The consular office shall put the registration stamp in the passport of the adopted child.

5. At the will of the adoptive parents the registration of the adopted child may be executed before the child's exit out of the Russian Federation through the Department of Consular service of the Ministry of Foreign Affairs of the Russian Federation.

In this case the specified department shall transmit the petition of the adoptive parents for the adopted child's registration, the child's registration card and the photographs to the consular office corresponding to the place of residence of the adoptive parents and shall put the registration stamp in the Passport of the child.

6. If the place of residence of the adoptive child has changed the adoptive parents shall inform the consular office at which this child has been registered and to register the child at the consular office corresponding to the new place of residence.

7. The control over the registration of the adopted child at a consular office shall be executed by an adoption organization specially authorized by a foreign state that represent the interests of the prospective adoptive parents at the adoption proceedings within the Russian Federation under the established order.

8. For the purpose of providing the well-timed registration of the adopted children at Consular Offices the Federal Operator of Databank of Children of the Russian Federation directs the information about the adopted children to them every 6 months.

At the end of the official year, consular offices shall transmit the lists of children registered under these Rules to the Federal Operator of Databank of Children of the Russian Federation and also inform them about the violation of the rights and legitimate interests of the adopted child and the unfavorable situation in the family of the adoptive parents.

Chapter Eight

Helpful Hints and Tips (FAQ's)

The following are common questions, mostly general in scope. Please keep in mind that the answers to these types of questions may vary with each case/individual. These answers tend to provide the most commonly accurate response to the question. Of course, it is impossible to list every question and answer imaginable, but if you are seeking answers to more specific questions either ask your adoption professional or research from the listings included in the back of this book. You may also want to keep in mind that the Russian adoption processes can change and what is accurate information today can become outdated or altered in the future.

Q. Can I get information about a "particular" child who is in the "particular" Orphanage in the "particular" Region?

A. According to the Federal Law about the State Databank of Children Without Parental Custody (articles 11 and 12). The information on children must be kept confidential except as outlined in these Articles.

Q. Can I adopt a child that has siblings without having to adopt the sibling(s)?

A. Yes, if it is determined by the Judge to be in the best interest of the child (Article 124 clause 3 of the Family Code).

Q. There are many children in Russian Orphanages, are they all available for adoption by foreign people?

A. No, there are many children in Russian orphanages who are not available for adoption. Many children are placed in orphanages on a temporary basis. Children available for adoption must be on the Database of Children Without Parental Custody for the required length of time to be eligible for adoption by foreign people. (Article 124 clause 4 of the Family Code).

Q. Are there age requirements for adoptive parents?

A. The Russian law has no limitations other than being of legal age as a parent. There is, however, a requirement specifying the difference of the age between a single adoptive parent and the child be at least 16 years (Article 127 clause 1 and Article 128 of the Family Code).

Q. Once I accept my referral, can anyone take the child prior to the Court granting the adoption?

A. Yes, a member of the child's family can petition to take custody of the child. Also any Russian citizens, who meets an established set of requirements will have priority to adopt this or any child, take them into guardianship (trusteeship) or foster care (Article 124 Clause 4 of the Family Code). At the same time, if the Federal/Regional

Operator of the Databank of Children provided a referral to a person (family) to visit a child, the Federal/Regional Operator is prohibited to disclose the information about the same child to another person (family) (Article 16 of The Rules of Keeping the State Databank of Children Without Parental Custody and its Formation and Use Control).

Q. Is it faster to adopt with an agency versus adopting independently?

A. No. The length of time an adoption takes is totally dependent on a variety of circumstances which are unrelated to your representation.

Q. I am single, can I adopt in Russia?

A. Yes. Russian Laws do not specify that a person must be married (Article 127 clause 1 of the Family Code).

Q. If my adoption is not granted by the Judge, what can I do legally?

A. You have the right to appeal the Court decision to a superior Court (Article 282 of the Code of Civil Procedure of the Russian Federation).

Q. What is the age limit for adopting in Russia?

A. No age limit is specified by Russian law (except that you must be over 18 years of age).

Q. How many trips do I have to make to Russia for my adoption?

A. There is no law indicating the number of trips required

to complete an adoption. However, two trips are necessary in most cases. During the first trip you will obtain a referral from the Regional or Federal Operator of the Databank of Children and meet a child. During the second trip you will attend the Court hearing. The amount of time between the first and second trip varies depending on the specific details of your case.

Q. How long do I need to stay in Russia for each trip?

A. The first trip can last as little as two days in some regions up to four or five days in other regions, depending on whether or not you accept your referral. The second trip can last for as little as two or three days up to 15 days, if you are required to stay for the 10 day "appeal period". The final stage of the adoption requires you to process out of the US Embassy in Moscow (or consulate in Vladivostok). The time required for this final procedure is usually just a few days. Of course, this can vary depending on weekends and holidays. Always plan on the fact you may need more time. Note: Only one parent needs to go on the first trip; both must be in Court (when there are two parents adopting).

Q. Do I have to donate to an orphanage?

A. No, it is not required by law or any legislation, however, most adopting parents do choose to give something that is needed by the orphanage.

Q. What is appropriate to donate to an orphanage?

A. It is best to talk directly with your adoption representative or the Director of the Orphanage prior to making any donation plans. Each orphanage may have different needs. If you donate cash, it should be done according to the laws of Russia, never "under the table" or without proper documentation.

Q. Is it appropriate to give gifts?

A. It is not necessary, but it is appropriate.

Q. What gifts are appropriate?

A. That is up to you, but never anything extravagant. For individuals, flowers, candy or other token gifts are appreciated. You may want to wait until traveling to Russia to purchase gifts.

Q. Homestudy: Is there a Russian accreditation requirement for my Homestudy agency?

A. There is no Russian accreditation requirement. Homestudies may be completed by any agency or social worker licensed by your State to provide this service.

Q. How do I know about the health of a child I am looking to adopt?

A. You will have permission, when visiting a child at the orphanage, to view medical records and you may also have an independent physician evaluate the child and/or the child's health information for the child prior to acceptance.

Q. Can I be specific about the child I am looking to adopt (age, sex, health, color of hair/skin, etc.)?

A. Yes, but the more flexible you are the better your chances to receive a referral to meet a child.

Q. What are the ages of children available for foreign Adoption in Russia?

A. Children from about 5 months up to the legal age of 18 are available (Article 124 clause 1 of the Family Code).

Q. Can anyone place a "hold" on a child I may be interested in adopting?

A. Until all of the necessary documents (your dossier) are submitted and accepted by the proper government officials for a specific child, this child would be considered by law adoptable by any qualified person. (Article 12, section 1, paragraph 3 of the Federal Law about the State Databank of Children Without Parental Custody).

Q. If I adopt and there is a problem, can the adoption be annulled?

A. Yes. You must petition the District Court in the region where the adoption was granted. This is a very rare occurrence according to statistics. (Article 282 of the Code of Civil Procedure).

Q. What is the "10-day waiting period" for in Russia?

A. This is the law for all civil cases, including adoption, and is commonly referred to as the "appeal time".

Q. Can I get a waiver for the 10 day required wait after my adoption is completed?

A. It is up to the Judge, but if presented properly showing cause, it is often granted (Article 211 clause 3 of Code of Civil Procedure).

Q. When I receive a referral, do I have to accept this child for adoption?

A. No, you have the right to refuse any child and can seek another referral.

Q. Do both parents have to travel to Russia?

A. It is only necessary for one parent to travel to obtain the referral and to meet the child (first trip). For the Court date, both parents must travel and be present in the courtroom.

Q. What should we wear to Court?

A. Always dress appropriate as you would in any Court of Law. Nothing casual, I recommend suit or coat and tie for men and dress or dress slacks for women.

Q. Is a Russian visa required for travel to Russia? How do we get this?

A. Yes, you will need a visa if you are not a Russian citizen and hold a Russian passport. You can get a visa through a number of international travel agencies and visa offices.

Q. How much money should I bring, can I use credit cards?

A. Not a simple question, but the best answer here is bring what you intend to spend with some extra just in case. If you will take sightseeing tours, shop or plan on an extended stay, bring more. If you need to get in and out of Russia in a short time, a minimal amount is necessary. Be sure to keep in mind any major expenses (i.e. airfare/hotels) that you will have to pay for as well as money for any INS related fees. Not all hotels and means of travel will take credit cards, so do not count on these. Traveler's checks are usually accepted, but fees may apply for exchange. You should not have any problems if you think through things and carry a little extra for the unexpected. If you are totally unsure, try to contact others that have recently traveled to your destination. Use a money belt or other safety device for security and be sure to declare the currency that you bring into Russia.

Chapter Nine
Common Russian Names and Nicknames

Female

Albina - (from Latin) white; derivatives – Albinka.

Aleutina - (from Greek) reflection, bad is alien to her nature; derivatives - Aleutina

Alexandra - (from Greek) a brave protector of people; derivatives – Sasha, Shura.

Alica (Alice) - (from Old German) noble estate; derivatives – Aliska.

Alina - (from Old German) noble; derivatives – Alinka.

Alla - (from Old Arabic) Sunday; derivatives - Ala, Alia.

Anastasia - (from Greek) risen from the dead; derivatives – Nastya, Nastusha, Nastyona.

Anfica - (from Greek) blooming.

Angelina - (from Greek) a messenger; the European variant of a name - Angela and Angelica; derivatives - Angelinka, Gelia, Gela.

Anna - (from Hebrew) blessing, merciful; derivatives - Annochka, Annushka, Nura, Anuta.

Antonina - (from Latin) verbose; derivatives – Tonya, Nusia.

Barbara - (from Latin) a foreigner.

Bella - (from Latin) beauty; derivatives – Bellia, Bella.

Capitolina - (from Latin) Capitol (the hill in Rome); derivatives – Capa, Capulia, Capusha,

Carina – (from Latin) looking forward.

Christina - (from Greek) devoted to Christ.

Clara - (from Latin) serene; derivatives – Clarka, Lara.

Claudia - (from Latin) lame; derivatives – Clava, Clasha.

Cleopatra - (from Greek) glory of the father.

Dana - (from Slavic) given, granted.

Daria - (from Persian) a great fire; derivatives – Darukha, Darusha.

Diana - (from Greek) divine; derivatives – Dianka, Dina, Diya, Ana, Anya.

Ekaterina - (from Greek) purity; derivatives – Katerina, Katya, Katukha, Katusha.

Elena - (from Greek) chosen one, bright, shining; derivatives – Alyona, Alyonka, Alyonushka, Lena, Lenochka, Lenchik.

Elisaveta (Elisabeth) - (from Hebrew) God's oath; derivatives – Veta, Liza, Lizaveta.

Ella - (from German) bright.

Elvira - (from German) a protector of people.

Emilia, Emma - (from Greek) flattering, affectionate; derivatives – Ema.

Eugenia - (from Greek) noble; derivatives – Zhenya.

Eva - (from Hebrew) life, derivatives - Evka.

Galina - (from Greek) quiet, serene; derivatives – Galinka, Galia, Gala.

Inga - (from Old Scandinavian) winter; the European variant of a name - **Ingeborga; Ingeborg**; derivatives – Ingusha.

Inna - (from Latin) a crying, rough flow; the European variant of a name: Innessa; derivatives: Innushka, Ina, Innusia, Innulia.

Iriada - (from Greek) a heroine; derivatives - Ira, Irishka, Irisha.

Irina (Irene) - (from Greek) peace; derivatives – Irinka, Irisha, Irishka, Ira, Irunia, Irusia.

Irma - (from Old German) fair.

Isabella - (from Spanish) beauty; derivatives – Bella, Bela.

Julietta - (from Latin) born in July; derivatives - Julia, Zhulia, Yulia, Yula.

Ksenia - (from Greek) hospitality, a foreigner; derivatives – Ksuta, Ksusha.

Lada - (from Old Russian) favorite, darling; derivatives – Ladusia, Ladushka.

Larisa - (from Greek) sweet, pleasant; (from Latin) seagull; derivatives – Lariska, Lara, Lora.

Laura - (from Latin) a bay tree; derivatives - Laurka, Lara.

Lidia - (from Greek) the name of an area in Small Asia; derivatives – Lida.

Lika - (from Greek) sweet.

Lilia - (from Latin) a white flower.

Linda - (from Spanish) beautiful.

Liya - (from Hebrew) an antelope; derivatives – Liika, Lilia.

Lolita - (from Spanish) grief, sorrow.

Louisa - (from Hebrew) God helped; the ex - German variant - Elisabeth; derivatives – Louiska, Liza.

Lubov - (from Old Slavic) love; derivatives – Luba, Lubasha, Lubusia, Lubashka.

Ludmila - (from Old Russian) nice, loved by people; derivatives – Ludmilka, Luda, Lusia, Mila.

Margarita (Margaret) - (from Latin) pearl; derivatives – Margaritka, Rita,

Marianna - from the names Maria and Anna; derivatives – Marianka.

Marina - (from Latin) from the sea, sea-born; derivatives – Marinka, Marisha.

Maria - (from Hebrew) bitter, sad, rejecting; derivatives – Masha.

Martha - (from Aramaic) a madam, a sovereign.

Maya - (from Greek) name of the ancient Greek goddess, mother of Hermes (Mercury); original mother of the Universe; derivatives – Mayunia, Mayukha.

Nadezhda - (from Slavic) hope; derivatives – Nadia, Nadukha, Nadusha, Nadushka.

Natalia - (from Latin) darling, a relative; derivatives – Natasha, Natusia.

Nelly - (from Greek) bright; derivatives – Nellia.

Nika - (from Greek) a victory.

Nina - (from Greek) named after the founder of the Syrian State Ninos; derivatives – Ninka, Ninulia.

Nonna - (from Latin) ninth; (from Greek) perspicacious.

Olga - (from Old Scandinavian) sainted, great; derivatives – Olya, Olunia, Olenka.

Paulina - (from Greek) significant; (from Latin) small; derivatives – Paulinka, Paulia.

Raica - (from Greek) easy; derivatives – Raya.

Regina - (from Latin) an empress.

Renata - (from Latin) restored to life; derivatives – Rena, Nata.

Rimma - (from Latin) throwing; (from Hebrew) an apple; derivatives – Rimmushka, Rimmulia, Rima.

Rosa - (from Latin) a rose; derivatives – Rosochka.

Roxana - (from Persian) a foreteller; derivatives – Roxanka.

Sara - (from Hebrew) noble.

Seraphima - (from Hebrew) ardent; derivatives – Sima, Simulia, Simunia.

Sophia - (from Greek) wisdom; derivatives – Sophiushka, Sonia, Sonusha.

Svetlana - (from Old Russian) bright; derivatives – Svetlanka, Sveta, Svetik, Svetulia, Lana.

Taisia - (from Greek) belonging to Izida (goddess of fertility, water, wind, and navigation); derivatives – Tasia, Taya.

Tamara - (from Hebrew) a Phoenician palm; derivatives – Tamarka, Toma, Tomulia.

Tatiana - (from Greek) an organizer; (from Latin) named after king **Tatty**; derivatives - Tatianka, Tania, Tanukha, Tanusha.

Uliana - (from Roman) from a personal name; derivatives – Ulia, Uliasha, Liana, Yana.

Valentina - (from Latin) strong, healthy; derivatives - Valentinka, Valya, Valusha.

Valeria - (from Latin) strong; derivatives – Lera.

Vanda - (from Old Slavic) a troublemaker, an arguer; derivatives – Vandochka, Vana.

Varvara - (from Latin) cruel, rough; (from Greek) a foreigner; derivatives – Varvarka, Varya.

Vera - (from Old Slavic) faith, belief; derivatives – Verulia, Verunia, Verusha.

Veronica - (from Greek) bringing a victory; (from Latin) a true, original image; derivatives - Veronichka, Vera, Verunia, Verusha.

Victoria - (from Latin) victory; derivatives - Vicka, Vickusha, Vita.

Violetta - (from Latin) a violet; derivatives – Viola, Vetta, Vittulia.

Yulia (Julia) - (from Greek) wavy, fluffy; (from Latin) a female Roman name.

Yana, Yanina - (from Hebrew) God's favor; derivatives – Yanka, Yanusia.

Zhanna - (from Hebrew) God's favor; derivatives – Zhanka, Zhanusia.

Zinaida - (from Greek) from the family of Zeus, like a goddess; derivatives – Zina, Zinakha, Zinulia, Zinusia, Zinia.

Zoya - (from Greek) life; derivatives – Zoika, Zoinka.

Male

Alexander - (from Greek) a brave protector; derivatives –
Sasha, Sania, Sashulia, Shura.

Alexey - (from Greek) a protector; derivatives – Lyosha,
Alyosha.

Anatoliy - (from Greek) eastern, rising; derivatives – Tolia,
Tolik.

Andrew - (from Greek) courageous, brave; derivatives -
Andrusha.

Anicim - (from Greek) performance, completion.

Antip - (from Greek) an opponent, an enemy.

Anton - (from Greek) an opponent, an enemy; (from Latin)
broad, derivatives – Antokha, Antosha.

Arcadiy - (from Greek) born as Arcadiy, rather verbose; derivatives – Arcasha.

Arkhip - (from Greek) a chief over horses; derivatives –
Arkhipka.

Arnold - (from Old Scandinavian) a singer; derivatives –
Arnoldik, Arnosha.

Arthemiy - (from Greek) safe, healthy; derivatives – Artem,
Tyoma.

Arthur - (from Celtic) a bear.

Boris - (from Old Slavic) Borislav – a fighter for glory; derivatives – Boriska, Borya.

Clim - (from Greek) a vine.

Daniel - (from Hebrew) my Judge is God; derivatives – Danilka.

David - (from Hebrew) favorite; derivatives – Davidka.

Denis - (from Greek) belonging to Dionysus; derivatives – Deniska, Denia.

Dmitriy - (from Greek) related to Demetra; derivatives – Dima, Dimukha, Dimusha, Dimulia, Mitya, Mitusha.

Edward - (from Old German) guard of riches; derivatives – Edik.

Efrem - (from Hebrew) prolific, productive; derivatives – Efremka, Rema.

Egor - (from Greek) a farmer; derivatives – Egorka, Zhora, Gosha.

Elisey - (from Hebrew) rescued by God.

Emelian - (from Greek) flattering; derivatives – Emeliasha, Emelia.

Emil - (from Latin) assiduous; derivatives – Milya.

Ephim - (from Greek) pious; derivatives – Ephimka, Phima.

Erick - (from Old Scandinavian) a noble leader.

Ermolay - (from Greek) people and Hermes; derivatives – Ermola, Ermosha.

Erofey - (from Greek) sanctified by God.

Eugeniy (Eugene) - (from Greek) noble; derivatives – Genya, Zhenya.

Fedot - (from Greek) given by the gods; derivatives – Fedot-ka, Fedya, Dotya.

Fyodor - (from Greek) God's gift; derivatives – Fedya, Fedusha.

Gavriil (Gabriel) - (from Hebrew) my power is God; derivatives – Gavrilka, Gavrukha, Gavrusha.

Gennadiy - (from Greek) noble; derivatives - Gena, Genia, Gesha.

Georgiy (George) - (from Greek) a farmer; derivatives – Zhora, Gera, Gesha, Gosha, Egor.

Gleb - (from Old Scandinavian) a favorite of Gods; derivatives – Glebushka.

Grigoriy (Gregory) - (from Greek) cheerful; derivatives – Grisha, Grishunia, Grinia.

Henry - (from Old German) powerful, rich; derivatives – Gena, Gera.

Ignatiy - (from Greek) unknown, a stranger; (from Latin) unborn; derivatives – Ignat.

Igor - (from Old Scandinavian) aggressive; derivatives – Igoryok, Igoryosha, Goga.

Ilya - (from Hebrew) God's fortress; derivatives – Ilukha, Ilusha.

Ivan - (from Hebrew) God's favor; derivatives – Vanya, Ivanushka.

Kirill (Cyril) - (from Greek) younger master; derivatives – Kirilka, Kiria, Kira, Kirukha, Kirusha.

Kondratiy - (from Greek) a soldier, carrying a spear; (from Latin) quadrangular; derivatives – Kondratka.

Konstantine - (from Latin) firm, steady; derivatives – Kostya, Kostik, Kostusha.

Kuzma - (from Greek) peace, decoration; derivatives – Kuzya.

Leonid - (from Greek) similar to a lion; derivatives – Lyonya.

Leontiy - (from Greek) a lion's one.

Lev (Leo) - (from Greek) a lion, a king of animals; derivatives – Lyovushka.

Makar - (from Greek) blissful, happy; derivatives – Makarka.

Maxim (from Latin) greatest; derivatives – Max, Maximka.

Mikhail (Michael) - (from Hebrew) equal to God; derivatives – Misha, Mishanya.

Miroslav - (from Old Slavic) glorifying the peace; derivatives – Mira, Slava.

Mitrophan - (from Greek) found by the mother; derivatives – Mitrophanka, Mitrophasha, Mitrokha.

Nazar - (from Hebrew) devoted to God; derivatives – Nazarka.

Nikiphor - (from Greek) victorious; derivatives – Nikisha, Nika.

Nikita - (from Greek) a winner; derivatives – Nikitka, Nika, Mikita.

Nikolay- (from Greek) a winner of the people; derivatives – Nikolasha, Kolya, Kolunya, Kolusia, Koliasha.

Oleg - (from Old Scandinavian) sainted; derivatives – Olezhek.

Pavel - (from Latin) small; derivatives – Pavlik, Pavlusha, Pasha.

Peter - (from Greek) a stone; derivatives – Petrusha, Petya.

Philip - (from Greek) loves horses; derivatives – Philipka, Philia, Philukha, Philusha.

Prochor - (from Greek) one who is in front of the chorus; derivatives – Prochorka, Prosha, Pronya.

Renat - (from Latin) restored to life.

Robert - (from Old German) undying fame.

Rodion - (from Greek) song for the ruler; derivatives – Rodia.

Roman - (from Latin) a Roman; derivatives – Romanka, Romasha, Romanya, Roma, Romulya.

Rostislav - (from Old Slavic) growing fame; derivatives – Rostya, Rostik.

Ruslan - (from Turkic) a lion; derivatives – Ruslanka, Ruslanchik.

Saveliy- (from Hebrew)   asked from God; derivatives – Savelushka, Sava.

Semyon - (from Hebrew) has heard; derivatives – Semyonka, Syoma, Senya, Senechka.

Seraphim - (from Hebrew)   burning, fiery; derivatives – Seraphimka, Sima, Simulia, Phima.

Sergey - (from Latin)   high, high-ranking; derivatives – Sergeyka, Sernulia, Sergunia, Seryozha.

Stanislav - (from Polish)   very nice, greatest; derivatives – Stas, Stasik.

Stephan - (from Greek)   a wreath; derivatives – Stephanka, Stephasha, Styopa.

Svyatoslav - (from Old Slavic)   sainted, glory; derivatives – Svyatoslavka, Slava, Slavik.

Taras - (from Greek)   to get to confusion, to disturb; derivatives – Taraska, Tarasik.

Tikhon - (from Greek)   successful; derivatives – Tisha.

Timothy - (from Greek)   esteeming God; derivatives – Timopheika, Timokha, Timosha, Tima

Timur - (from Turkic)   made of iron; derivatives – Timurka.

Trophim - (from Greek)   a supporter; derivatives – Trophimka, Trokha, Trosha.

Vadim - (from Old Russian)   to accuse, to slander; derivatives – Vadimka, Dima, Vadya.

Valentine - (from Latin)   strong, healthy; derivatives – Valia.

Valeriy - (from Latin) strong, healthy; derivatives – Valera.

Vasiliy- (from Greek) a tsar, a king; derivatives – Vasya.

Veniamin - (from Hebrew) the favorite son; derivatives – Venia.

Victor - (from Latin) a winner; derivatives – Vitya, Vitukha, Vitusha.

Vitaliy - (from Latin) live; derivatives – Vitalia, Vitalik.

Vladimir - (from Old Slavic) to rule the world; derivatives – Volodya, Vova.

Vladislav - (from Serbian) possessing glory; derivatives – Slava, Slavik, Slavunya, Slavusia, Vladia, Ladia, Vadia.

Vsevolod - (from Old Russian) all-powerful; derivatives: Seva.

Vyacheslav- (from Old Russian) a great glory; derivatives: Slava.

Yakov (Jacob) - (from Hebrew) next; derivatives: Yacusha, Yasha.

Yan (Jan) - (from Hebrew) God's favor.

Yaroslav - (from Old Slavic) furious, glory, glorifying Jarrila, god of the sun; derivatives: Yaroslavka, Slava, Slavunya, Slavusia, Rosia.

Chapter Ten
Helpful Russian Words and Phrases

Words

Airplane	*samalyot*	Bee	*pchela*
Airport	*aeraport*	Belt	*remeyn*
Alphabet	*alfa veet*	Bicycle	*velaseepyed*
Angry	*syerdeetye*	Big	*balshoy*
Apple	*yablaka*	Bird	*pteetsa*
Aunt	*tyotya*	Black	*chyornay*
		Blanket	*adee yala*
Baby	*re byo nak*	Blouse	*bloozka*
Bad	*pla khoy*	Blue	*seenee*
Ball	*myach*	Bone	*kost*
Banana	*ba nan*	Book	*kneega*
Bandage	*beent*	Books	*kneegee*
Basketball	*baskyetbol*	Boots	*sapa gee*
Bath	*vanna*	Boys	*malcheekee*
Bathtub	*vanna*	Bread	*khlyeb*
Beans	*fasol*	Breakfast	*zavtrak*
Beautiful	*krasyeve*	Broom	*vyenik*
Bed	*kravat*	Brother	*brat*
Beer	*peeva*	Brown	*kareechnyvy*
Bedroom	*spalnya*	Bus	*avtoboos*

Cabbage	*kapoosta*	Dirty	*gryazny*
Cake	*tort*	Doctor	*vrach*
Camera	*foto aparat*	Dog	*sabaka*
Candle	*svyechka*	Doll	*koo kla*
Car	*masheena*	Dolls	*kookly*
Carpet	*kavyor*	Door	*dver*
Carrot	*markov*	Downstairs	*vneezoo*
Carry	*naseet*	Dress	*platye*
Cat	*koshka*	Drink	*peet*
Chair	*kryeslo*	Dry	*sookhoy*
Cheese	*syr*	Duck	*ootka*
Chest (body)	*grood*		
Chicken	*kooreetsa*	Ears	*ooshee*
Children	*dyetee*	Easy	*lekh ko*
Chocolate	*shakalad*	Eat	*kushat*
Church	*tsyerkov*	Eggs	*yaytsa*
Circle	*kroog*	Elbow	*lokat*
Clean	*cheesty*	Eye	*glaz*
Clothes	*adyezhda*	Eyeglasses	*ochkee*
Clouds	*oblaka*		
Coat	*palto*	Face	*leetso*
Cold	*kholodny*	Fall (season)	*oyseen*
Comb	*raschyoska*	Family	*semya*
Cow	*karova*	Far	*dalyeko*
Cucumber	*agooryets*	Farm	*fyerma*
		Fast	*beystra*
Dad	*papa*	Fat	*tolsty*
Dance	*tanseyvat*	Father	*atyets*
Daughter	*doch*	Feet and legs	*nogee*
Dead	*myortvy*	Fence	*zabor*
Dentist	*zoobnoy vrach*	A few	*nyeskolko*
Desk	*parta, stol*	Fight	*dratsa*
Difficult	*troodna*	Fight (playing)	*barotsa*
Dinner	*oozhyen*	Fingers	*paltsy*

Helpful Russian Words and Phrases

Fish	*reeba*	I	*ya*
Flour	*mooka*	Ice	*lyod*
Flowers	*tsvety*	Ice cream	*marozhnoya*
Fly (bug)	*mookha*	Inside	*vh*
Football	*footbol*		
Forest	*lyes*	Jacket	*peedzhak*
Forks	*veelkee*	Jelly	*zhyelye*
Fruit	*frookty*	Juice	*sok*
Frying pan	*skavarodka*	Jump	*priguy*
Funny	*smyshnoy*		
		Key	*klooch*
Girls	*dyevochkee*	Kind	*dobrye*
Glass (drinking)	*stakan*	Kiss	*patsalooy*
Gloves	*pyerchatkee*	Kitchen	*kookhnya*
Go	*idi*	Kitten	*katyona*
Good	*kharashaw*	Knee	*kalyena*
Grandfather	*dye dooshka*	Knees	*kalyenee*
Grandmother	*ba booshka*		
Grapefruit	*gryeypfroot*	Lake	*ozyera*
Grapes	*veenagrad*	Lamp	*lampa*
Grass	*trava*	Left	*levye*
Green	*zyelyony*	Lemon	*leemon*
Grey	*syery*	Lips	*gooby*
		Living room	*gasteenaya*
Hair	*volasee*	Love	*lubov*
Head	*galava*	Lunch	*abyed*
High	*vysokee*		
Horse	*loshyad*	Man	*moozhcheena*
Hot	*garyachy*	Many	*mnoga*
Hotel	*gasteeneetsa*	Map	*karta*
House	*dom*	Me	*Ya*
Hungry	*golodnye*	My	*Moy, Mya, Myo*
Husband	*moozh*	Meat	*myasa*

Medicine	*lyekarstva*	Policeman	*meeleetsyanyer*
Milk	*malako*	Popcorn	*vazdooshnaya*
Mirror	*zyerkalo*		*kookoorooza*
Money	*dyengee*	Potato	*kartofyel*
Moon	*loona*	Presents	*padarkee*
Mother	*mat*		
Mouth	*rot*	Radio	*radeeo*
		Rain	*dozhd*
Neck	shyeya	Rainbow	*radooga*
No	*nyet*	Red	*krasny*
Nose	*nos*	Refrigerator	*khaladeelneek*
Nurse	*myedsyestra*	Rice	*rees*
		River	*ryeka*
Old	*stary*	Road	*daroga*
Onion	*look*	Roof	*krysha*
Open	*atkroy*	Rug	*kovreek*
Orange (color)	*aranzhyevy*	Run	*byegat*
Oranges	*apyelseemy*		
		Salad	*salat*
Pajamas	*peezhama*	Salt	*sol*
Pancakes	*aladee*	Sandals	*sandalee*
Paper	*boomaga*	Sandwich	*bootyerbrod*
Peach	*pyerseek*	School	*shkola*
Pencil	*karandash*	Scissors	*nozhneetsy*
Pepper	*pyeryets*	Shirt	*roobashka*
People	*lyoodee*	Shoes	*tooflee*
Photograph	*fatagrafeeya*	Short	*karotkee*
Piano	*pianeeno*	Shower	*doosh*
Picture	*karteena*	Silly	*gloopee*
Pillow	*padooshka*	Sink	*rakaveena*
Pineapple	*ananas*	Sister	*systra*
Pink	*rozavy*	Small	*malyenkee*
Plums	*sleevy*	Smart	*oolnee*
Pocket	*karman*	Snow	*snyeg*

Helpful Russian Words and Phrases

Soap	*meyla*	Toothbrush	*zoobnaya shyotka*
Socks	*naskee*		
Soft	*myakhkee*	Toothpaste	*zoobnaya pasta*
Spaghetti	*spagyettee*		
Spider	*paook*	Towel	*palatyentsye*
Spoon	*lozhka*	Toys	*eegrooshkee*
Sport	*sport*	Train	*poyezd*
Spring	*vesna*	Tree	*dyeryeva*
Stairs	*lyestneetsa*		
Stand	*stayat*	Uncle	*dyadya*
Star	*zvezda*	Under	*pwod*
Store	*magazeen*		
Strawberry	*kloobneeka*	Vegetables	*ovashchee*
Sugar	*sakhar*		
Summer	*lyeto*	Wall	*styena*
Sun	*solntsye*	Wash	*myt*
Swim	*plavat*	Water	*vada*
Swimsuit	*koopalnyk*	Wet	*mokry*
		White	*byely*
T-shirt	*footbolka*	Window	*akno*
Table	*stol*	Winter	*zeema*
Talk	*gavareet*	Woman	*zhyenshcheena*
Tea	*chy*		
Teddy bear	*myed vyezhonok*	Yellow	*zhyolty*
		Yes	*Da*
Telephone	*tyelyefon*	Yesterday	*Vchera*
Television	*tyelyeveezor*		
Thumb	*balshoy palyets*		
Today	*Sevodnya*		
Toilet	*ooneetaz*		
Tomatoes	*pameedory*		
Tomorrow	*zavtra*		
Tongue	*yazyk*		

Phrases

A little	*nem no go*
Are you cold	*tebye ho lodno*
Are you hot	*tebye zharko*
Are you hungry	*tea hochesh kushat*
Are you ok	*tebye haroshaw*
Are you tired (feminine)	*tea oostala*
Are you tired (masculine)	*tea oostal*
Be careful	*as ta rozh na*
Brush your teeth	*chees tee zoo be*
Bye	*paka*
Can I help you	*teb ye po moch*
Can you wait	*tea mozhesh padazhdat*
Do not be afraid	*ne boysa*
Do what I say	*dyeli shto ya gavaroo*
Do you feel sick	*teb ye ploho*
Do you like it	*teb ye nra veetsa*
Do you like to play	*tea lou beesh ig raat*
...............to draw	..................*re sa vaat*
...............to read	...................*che tat*
...............to sing	.......................*pet*
...............to watch TV	...................*smot ret tele vee zor*
Do you need to pee	*tea ho chesh pee sat*
Do you understand me	*tea menya po nee mayesh*
Do you want more	*tea ho chesh yesh yo*
Do you want to play	*tea ho chesh eeg raat*
...............to eat	.................*kushat*
...............to be outside	.................*goo lat*
...............to drink	.................*peet*
...............to sleep	.................*spaat*

Does this hurt	*etta baleet*
Give me your hand	*die rook oo*
Good morning	*dobro ye ootrah*
Good night	*spockoy nye nochee*
Goodbye	*das vidania*
Hello	*zdrastvoy*
Help me	*pa ma gee mne*
Her name is	*yeyo zo voot*
Hi	*privyet*
His name is	*yevo zo voot*
How do you say__in Russian	*kak skazat ___ po rooskie*
How much	*skol ka*
How	*kak*
I am angry	*ya ser zhoos*
I am your dad	*ya tvoy papa*
I am your mom	*ya tvo ya mama*
I don't know	*ya ne zhna yu*
I don't understand	*ya ne ponee ma yu*
I know	*ya zhna yu*
I love you	*ya tibya lu blu*
I understand	*ya ponee ma yu*
I'm Hungry (feminine)	*ya go lod naya*
I'm hungry (masculine)	*ya go lod nee*
I'm thirsty	*ya ho choo peet*
I'm tired (feminine)	*ya oostala*
I'm tired (masculine)	*ya oostal*
In English it is___	*po ungleeskie eta___*
It is good	*eta harashaw*
It is tasty	*eta vkoosna*
It's time to eat dinner	*pa ra oo zheenat*
It's time to go to bed	*pa ra spat*

Adopting In Russia

It's time to bathe	*pa ra myetsa*
Let's go	*posh lee*
Lie down	*la zhees*
Listen	*slew shy*
Look	*smot ree*
More	*yesh yo*
My name is	*men ya zo voot*
Open your mouth	*ot kroy rot*
Play quietly	*eeg rye tee ho*
Please	*pazhalusta*
Quiet	*tea she*
Show me	*paka zhi mne*
Sit down and play	*see dee ee eeg rye*
Sit down	*sa dees*
Sit here	*sa dees toot*
Sit in your chair	*sad na stool*
Sit there	*sa dees tum*
Soon	*sko row*
Stand here	*vstan toot*
Stand there	*vstan tum*
Stand up	*vstavaye*
Thank you very much	*spaseebo bolshoye*
Thank you	*spaseebo*
This is hot	*ga ree cho*
This is our cat	*eta nasha koshka*
This is our dog	*eta nasha so baka*

Helpful Russian Words and Phrases

Wait	*pa dozh dee*
Wash your face	*moy leet so*
Wash your hands	*moy roo kee*
We are going to_____	*me idyom _____*
We love you	*me tibya lu bim*
What did you say	*shto tea ska zal (a)*
What is that	*shto eta*
What is your name	*kak tebya zo voot*
What	*shto*
What's wrong	*shto ne tak*
When	*kogda*
Where does it hurt	*gde bol eet*
Where is the bathroom	*gde too ah let*
Where to	*kooda*
Where	*gde*
Who	*kto*
Why are you crying	*po che moo tea plachesh*
Why	*pochee moo*
You are welcome	*puzhalsta*
You need a bath	*teb ye noozh no meet sa*

Chapter Eleven

Useful Information

Informational Websites

http://usembassy.state.gov/posts/rs1/wwwhcm.html

http://russianadoption.org Great site with a wealth of information for those who have lots of time to devote to research.

http://www.adopting.com/start.html Another good web site with adoption information.

http://www.calib.com/naic/ National Adoption Information Clearing House.

http://www.ibar.com/voices/forums/boards/index.html A place where adoptive parents and potential adoptive parents can go if they have adopted or plan to adopt in Russia.

http://travel.state.gov/children's_issues.html US Department of State, The Office of Children's Issues.

http://www.ins.usdoj.gov/graphics/formsfee/forms/index.htm
INS Forms and fees

http://www.ins.gov/graphics/publicaffairs/factsheets/chowto. htm Getting US Citizenship for your child.

http://usembassy.state.gov/posts/rs1/wwwhcm.html Site for Basic Embassy information (Address, contact numbers, hours of operation, holidays, etc.)

http://www.law.cornell.edu/topics/Table_Adoption.htm (State Adoption Laws)

http://www.ed.gov.ru/sch-edu/chil-s/accred.html Ministry of Education of the Russian Federation (Moscow) web site listing accredited adoption organizations of foreign countries. Site is partially in Russian, but organizations are in English.

http://map.rin.ru/index_e.html Great map site with regional listings.

http://russianadoption.org/Canadian%20agencies.htm Canadian Agencies and information resources.

http://www.hrw.org/campaigns/russia98/index.htm Human rights watch as it pertains to Russian orphanages.

http://www.comeunity.com/adoption/health/clinics.html Directory of clinics and doctors in the US and Canada specializing in International adoption health issues.

http://www.russianfoods.com/ Website that includes Russian recipes/food and more.

http://www.irs.gov/file/display/0,,i1%3D52%26generi-cId%3D16260,00.html This is the site for the latest on US Adoption Tax Credit information.

Russian Adoption Discussion Boards

Adoption discussion boards on the internet can provide a wealth of great information and support for those families interested in adoption. It can also provide a wonderful way to communicate with others and discuss common issues that are of specific interest to the reader.

You should exercise caution when reading information from message boards or from web sites. Be sure you can verify the sources of the information you seek. Many people post with good intentions about their own experience (good or bad) but it can often be an isolated case or incident. One must read these as informational pieces rather than factual pertaining to all adoptions.

Below are a few of the many boards available for those seeking Russian or foreign adoption.

http://eeadopt.org The A-PARENT-RUSS mailing list is for parents who are either interested in adopting or have adopted children from Russia or from one of the republics that used to be part of the former Soviet Union.

http://www.frua.org Families for Russian and Ukrainian Adoption (FRUA) is an international support network of and for families who have adopted or are in the process of adopting from the former Soviet Union and Eastern Europe. With 37 regional chapters and contacts, our mission is to support the whole life experience of Eastern European orphan children and to strengthen the families that are created through adoption.

http://groups.yahoo.com/group/Ind_Russian_Adopt/ Yahoo [Groups] contain several other topical discussion boards for Russian Adoption that are even more specific to areas of Russia. These boards can be extremely helpful in gathering information or simply talking with those that are somewhere in the process. The above referenced site is for those interested in Independent Adoption. You must first register in Yahoo before you can access the discussion groups. Each group you access will require registration. Registration is free.

http://www.russianadoption.org Russian Adoption Medical Services discussion board.

Embassy Websites in Moscow:

http://www.europanas.com/Argentina-Rusia-en.htm
Argentina Embassy website in Moscow

http://www.australianembassy.ru/index.htm
Australian Embassy website in Moscow

http://www.britemb.msk.ru/consular/index_ie.htm
British Embassy website covering adoptions in Russia (basic information)

http://www.canadaeuropa.gc.ca/country_rus-e.asp
(informational web site, not an official Embassy web site) Canadian Embassy in Moscow, Russia 23 Starokonyushenny Pereulok, Moscow, 121002 Russia Tel: 9566666 Fax: 2329948 E-mail: mosco@mosco01.x400.gc.ca

http://www.finemb-moscow.fi/
Finnish Embassy website in Moscow

http://www.ambafrance.ru/rus/index.asp
French Embassy website in Moscow

http://www.deutschebotschaft-moskau.ru/
German Embassy website in Moscow

http://www.nzembassy.msk.ru/index.html
New Zealand Embassy website in Moscow

http://www.sweden.ru/rus/index.htm
Swedish Embassy website in Moscow

http://www.ispania.aha.ru/
Spain Embassy website in Moscow

http://usembassy.state.gov/moscow/
United States of America Embassy in Moscow

Note: **No endorsement of published websites or their content by the author. Sites provided are for personal research and reading purposes only.**

Conversion Tables

Distance

1 Kilometers = 0.62140 Miles	1 Feet = 30.48000 Centimeters
1 Miles = 1.60900 Kilometers	1 Centimeters = 0.03281 Feet
1 Yards = 0.91440 Meters	1 Inches = 2.54000 Centimeters
1 Meter = 1.09360 Yards	1 Centimeters = 0.39370 Inches
1 Meters = 3.28100 Feet	1 Inches = 25 Millimeters
1 Feet = 0.30480 Meters	1 Millimeter = .04 Inches

Weight

1 Ounces = 30 Grams	1 Pound = .45 Kilograms
1 Gram = .035 Ounces	1 Kilogram = 2.2 Pounds
1 Pound = 454 Grams	1 Ounce = .028 Kilograms
1 Gram = .002 Pound	1 Kilogram = 35 Ounces

Liquids

1 US Gallons = 3.78500 Liters
1 Liters = 0.26420 US Gallons

1 US Liquid Quarts = 0.94640 Liters
1 Liters = 1.05700 US Liquid Quarts

1 Liters = 33.81000 Fluid Ounces
1 Fluid Ounces = 0.02957 Liters

Temperature

F/C	**F/C**
95/35	25/-4
90/32	15/-9
85/29	5/-15
80/27	0/-18
75/24	-10/-23
70/21	-20/-29
60/16	-30/-34
50/10	-40/-40
40/4	-50/-46
32/0	

Russian Regions

Article 65 of the Constitution of the Russian Federation:

The Russian Federation shall consist of the subjects of the Federation:

1. Republic of Adygeya (Adygeya)
2. Republic of Altai
3. Republic of Bashkortostan
4. Republic of Buryatia
5. Republic of Dagestan
6. Ingush Republic
7. Kabardin-Balkar Republic
8. Republic of Kalmykia — Khalmg Tangch
9. Karachayevo-Cherkess Republic
10. Republic of Karelia
11. Republic of Komi
12. Republic of Mari El
13. Republic of Mordovia
14. Republic of Sakha (Yakutia)
15. Republic of North Ossetia
16. Republic of Tatarstan (Tatarstan)
17. Republic of Tuva
18. Udmurt Republic
19. Republic of Khakasia
20. Chechen Republic
21. Chuvash Republic— Chavash Republics
22. Altai Territory
23. Krasnodar Territory
24. Krasnoyarsk Territory
25. Primorsk Territory
26. Stavropol Territory
27. Khabarovsk Territory
28. Amur regions
29. Arkhangelsk regions
30. Astrakhan regions
31. Belgorod regions
32. Bryansk regions
33. Vladimir regions
34. Volgograd regions
35. Vologda regions
36. Voronezh regions
37. Ivanovo regions
38. Irkutsk regions
39. Kaliningrad regions
40. Kaluga regions
41. Kamchatka regions

42. Kemerovo regions
43. Kirov regions
44. Kostroma regions
45. Kurgan regions
46. Kursk regions
47. Leningrad regions
48. Lipetsk regions
49. Magadan regions
50. Moscow regions
51. Murmansk regions
52. Nizhny Novgorod regions
53. Novgorod regions
54. Novosibirsk regions
55. Omsk regions
56. Orenburg regions
57. Oryol regions
58. Penza regions
59. Perm regions
60. Pskov regions
61. Rostov regions
62. Ryazan regions
63. Samara regions
64. Saratov regions
65. Sakhalin regions
66. Sverdlovsk regions
67. Smolensk regions
68. Tambov regions
69. Tver regions
70. Tomsk regions
71. Tula regions
72. Tyumen regions
73. Ulyanovsk regions
74. Chelyabinsk regions
75. Chita regions
76. Yaroslavl regions
77. Moscow - Federal city
78. St. Petersburg - Federal city
79. Jewish Autonomous regions
80. Aginsky Buryat Autonomous Area
81. Komi-Permyak Autonomous Area
82. Koryak Autonomous Area
83. Nenets Autonomous Area
84. Taimyr (Dolgan-Nenets) Autonomous Area
85. Ust-Ordynsky Buryat Autonomous Area
86. Khanty-Mansi Autonomous Area
87. Chukchi Autonomous Area
88. Evenk Autonomous Area
89. Yamal-Nenets Autonomous Area